Christmas
2000

Pull the door marked push

INSIDE THE HIGH IQ SOCIETY

ANNE SCHULMAN

ILLUSTRATED BY
MARTYN TURNER OF
THE IRISH TIMES

Published jointly by

MENSA PUBLICATIONS LIMITED

GRANTA EDITIONS

DEDICATION

To my husband David in love and friendship.

First published 1992
ISBN 0 906782 96 1

Published by Mensa Publications Limited, Mensa House,
St John's Square, Wolverhampton WV2 4AH, in association with
Granta Editions, 47 Norfolk Street, Cambridge CB1 2LE

Granta Editions is an imprint of The Book Concern Ltd

British Library Cataloguing in Publication Data
is available from the British Library

Design and production in association with
Book Production Consultants, Cambridge.

Printed and bound in Finland

Contents

Foreword

SIR CLIVE SINCLAIR

Mensa is a strange place. It shares a prime feature with Dr Who's Tardis: the inside bears no relation to the outside. I have been a member now for thirty-three years and find it hard to remember how I saw the society before I joined, but I see it a little through the eyes of others when I hear their comments. They expect, I think, a highly cerebral organisation devoted to the benefit of members perhaps at the expense of outsiders. In truth it is simply a very fine and very large social club which excludes from membership only those who cannot do well in rather odd tests.

That such an organisation should be successful is strange indeed, but it is – very. Membership now is over 100,000. Those who join almost always remain. It transcends divisions of taste, faith, race, sex, and national boundary. It is, in a word, a curiosity and I am delighted that here at last is a book which tells the story. I am especially delighted that this book has been written by the lovely and talented Anne Schulman, a friend of mine through Mensa for more years than either of us cares to admit.

Author's acknowledgements

Sincere thanks for their efficient 'search and rescue' to Ed Vincent, Executive Director, International Mensa; Harold Gale, Executive Director, British Mensa; Sheila Skolnik, Executive Director, American Mensa and Robert Allen, Editorial Director at Mensa Publications. I am deeply grateful to Clive Sinclair for his kind words and friendship; to Victor Serebriakoff, Honorary President, for his time and for his generosity in permitting the use of information from his book *Mensa: The Society for the Highly Intelligent* and to American Mensa for their equally generous permission to use information contained in *A History of Mensa*. To Simon Clark, Mark Griffin, Gabe Werber, Darlene Criss, Hans Fromer, Amy Shaughnessy, Elaine Kennedy, Carol Hilson, David Lally let me say, 'Thank you all for your kind help.' I should like to acknowledge my debt to all the Mensans who took the time and trouble to contribute in some way, and to all members everywhere; without them this book could not have been written. Last, but not least, I owe much to my family and friends for their patience, encouragement and faith in the dark days.

Introduction

Mensa, the high IQ society, provokes a variety of responses: admiration, terror, envy, faint-heartedness and, on occasion, derision.

This book, whilst not autobiographical, is one member's view of Mensa. I have over a period of several years lived with the Irish Chairman, the Irish President, a member of the British Mensa Committee and the International Chairman. Before you charge me with immorality, let me hasten to say they are all one and the same person, my husband. Because of his total involvement with Mensa I have become, by osmosis, an observer of this multi-faceted society.

Mensa is different things to different people. To some it is a wonderful social club, to others, a means of contacting people of similar and often specialised interests and, to the more isolated, it provides the opportunity to join in stimulating conversation not available in the normal course of their lives.

Many books are prefaced by a quotation; the one I have chosen for mine comes not from the Bard of Avon, but from an American paper-napkin company – 'Enjoy'.

Anne Schulman, 1992.

PART ONE

CHAPTER 1

Pre Mensa – true tension!

My husband, David, joined Mensa in 1978 and soon became involved with the Irish Mensa Committee. This encompasses both Northern Ireland and the Republic (a very happy union) and is a virtually autonomous body using the facilities of the British Mensa office. Shortly after this he was elected as a representative to the British Mensa Committee.

This position, needless to say, involved a lot of correspondence and telephone calls. I often acted as unofficial secretary to the various callers and my sympathy went out to one young man who appeared to have a most unfortunate speech impediment. His conversation went as follows: 'Hello, Anne, beep, beep, beep.' 'This is Dave, beep, beep, beep.' 'Is David there? beep, beep, beep.' It took me some time to realise that the reason for his odd speech pattern was that he was feeding small sums of money into a public telephone, so each call lasted about ten seconds. Teased unmercifully after this, David Lally, the official archivist and indefatigable worker for Mensa, took it all in good part and smiled enigmatically when it was suggested that the telephone was an integral part of his anatomy.

It was decided that a meeting of the British Mensa Committee would be held in Dublin to coincide with the Irish Mensa Annual Gathering. This was to be my first meeting with the awe-inspiring people about whom I had only heard and read: the Chairman, Clive Sinclair, whose inventive genius made daily headlines; Victor Serebriakoff, Honorary President of International Mensa, a man of infinite talent and Mensa's finest ambassador; and several other people, possibly not as well known, but equally respected.

Panic set in! My knowledge of computers and electronics was, to say the least, non-existent, and of the workings and personalities of Mensa, at best, sketchy. A cold or a mild attack of influenza would have been quite appealing at the time.

My fears proved groundless. Everyone was charming and friendly. On the first day several of us were having lunch in the Berkeley Court Hotel coffee shop and the conversation flowed. One of the topics discussed was the possibility of reducing the cost of launching rockets into space by using the same method as aircraft take-off. Aeronautics is not my first subject and it was at this point that my intelligence came to the rescue – I shut up.

Most of Mensa's major gatherings begin with an 'icebreaker', and the wearing of name tags, often with name of the member's town, state or country added, helps in the process of getting acquainted. New members soon discover other Mensans can be friendly, welcoming and have only one head, like everyone else.

The usual method of testing in the United Kingdom and Ireland is, in the first instance, an unsupervised test. Instructions are given as to how it should be approached and timed. The results are then assessed and the applicant informed. If the result approaches, or reaches, the required score the applicant is invited to take a supervised test, the result of which determines whether or not one is eligible for membership.

This has not always been the procedure. When David first applied for membership there was the unsupervised test, which one undertook to do unaided and in the time allowed. He completed and returned the test and, in due course, received a letter informing him that he was now eligible to join Mensa and that the relevant papers would follow shortly. Within a week they did arrive but were not quite the ones he had expected; they stated that due to an abnormally high number of people qualifying, it had been decided only to accept those who successfully completed a supervised test. Unfortunately, in the 1950s testing centres were few and far between; there were none in Ireland, where we were living, and so the papers were put into a box and forgotten.

Several years later he read in a newspaper article that Mensa in Ireland was alive and well, so he applied again. This time there were no problems and David became the first Mensan in the family.

The second was our daughter Lynda. Having successfully completed the 'home' test she was then invited to take the supervised one. She made her way to the vast university campus where the testing session was to take place. The venue had been changed and vague directions made it difficult to find the newly assigned room. With seconds to spare she grabbed the handle of the door and pulled. The door failed to budge. She pulled harder. And again. A gentleman inside the room watched through the glass-panelled door with amusement and then courteously opened it for her. 'If you want to become a member of Mensa you can't pull a door marked "Push",' he informed her. Happily this proved to be incorrect; nervousness works in mysterious ways. She is now married and her husband, Pat, is also a Mensan.

After I had decided to use Lynda's experience as the title for the book, I received a note wishing me good luck from Dr Madsen Pirie, Secretary of British Mensa and President of the Adam Smith Institute. He had explained the meaning of 'pull' and 'push' to a new French intern at the Institute and the next day had caught her with her fingers under the door marked 'Lift'.

Some time later, a long-forgotten incident produced the following erudite conversation at home. 'You are both stupid,' I accused. 'No we are not,' replied my husband, 'and we have certificates to prove it.' 'Neh, neh, neh, neh, neh,' added our sophisticated Mensan daughter. There was no answer to this. Or was there? Having for years resisted any attempt to take the test I decided in the end that the time had come to take the plunge. As I had never taken an IQ test before, I purchased a book on the subject. After looking through it I decided that, possibly, the best course of action would be to apologise to them both, hoping that they had not noticed my discomfort. However, somehow stubbornness took over and I started working my way through it. At first it appeared to be very difficult but, little by little, it became clearer.

Eventually the day of the test arrived. I set off with the good luck wishes of my family and advice from my husband not to leave any blank answers (all questions are multiple choice). As I drove along my courage and nerves were failing rapidly. Having done fairly well on the 'home' test, would I find the supervised test easier or more difficult? What were my qualifications? What excuse could I make if I failed to achieve the required standard?

When finally confronted by 'the test', for the first time in my life my mind was a total and utter blank (there are those who would disagree). It could have been written in hieroglyphics for all the sense it made. After what seemed an age, the mists began to clear and I worked my way through the pages until at last it was finished.

Life returned to normal and the ordeal was forgotten until one morning I saw an envelope bearing the Mensa emblem. This time it was addressed to me. Brimful of confidence I refused to open it and handed it to David, carefully watching his face. A broad grin appeared on it. For three days I carried that sheet of paper in my handbag until the thought struck me that if I lost it I might have to take another test.

The fourth member of the family, our son Paul, consistently refused to take the test, despite family teasing and gifts of 'Densa' tee-shirts, till he read an article which was Mensa inspired. It contained an IQ test, the result of which gave an indication of how one would fare in a formal test. His result was very encouraging and, more to please us than anything else, he agreed to take the official test. We were delighted when he, too, passed, making us a family of Mensans.

CHAPTER 2

Strangers on a train

Once upon a time long, long ago – in August 1945 to be exact – a remarkable event occurred. Two strangers travelling by train spoke to each other. In England this in itself is a near miracle, but more was to come. The elder of the two was an Australian, Roland Berrill, the younger, Lancelot Lionel Ware. They discussed intelligence and the consequences of being governed by people who lack that commodity. They came up with the suggestion that people of proven intelligence should form themselves into an organisation that could be called upon for advice when required. Although the aims and objects of the society were eventually more modest it was from this chance meeting that Mensa was founded.

Lancelot Ware was on his way to the enchanted city of Oxford to continue his graduate studies in law. Berrill, one of the city's dreaming squires and a non-practising barrister, was also journeying to the enchanted city, and there they took rooms in the same lodging-house. It was on that house, years later, that the city's elders erected a plaque proclaiming that this was Mensa's birthplace.

The chroniclers of the day tell us that Berrill was a most eccentric man, who at times could be intimidating. He undertook the challenging quest for members and scribed letters to his recruits informing them of the events they should attend.

As in all good tales, there was a queen – indeed, there were several. Mensa's 'queens' or '*corps d'esprit*' were beautiful maidens chosen to represent the Society or act as hostesses at grand and formal gatherings. One of their duties was to welcome new members. Berrill was a man of considerable means and it was his idea to appoint the queens. He bought and paid for the robes of the lucky (?) maidens. He insisted on supervising their investiture himself and, reluctantly, this was accepted. However, his luck ran out (and so, it is said, did the queen) when it was suggested that he perform the undressing prior to the ceremonial robing.

He appointed himself 'Secretary' of Mensa and proclaimed: 'There will be no committees.' He spent large sums of his own money and, had he not done so, Mensa would probably have ceased to exist. In the year of 1948 the first Annual Gathering was held. Berrill decreed that it would be residential. 'We all sleep under the same roof on the night of the first Saturday in November and take luncheon together on the Sunday.' The chosen venue was the Cumberland Hotel, situated at Marble Arch in London. This Annual Gathering has now become a tradition. The largest gathering recorded was held in New York, where 1,800 revellers joined in the celebrations.

Towards the end of 1949 a humble timber merchant applied to join the merry throng. His name was Victor Serebriakoff. He applied for an unsupervised test and was accepted for membership; it amused him to discover that there was, in fact, no supervised test (a harmless way to discourage cheating). It must be proclaimed from the mountain tops that Victor held Mensa together during the difficult years that followed. He is often referred to as the father of Mensa, and it is through his generosity that I recount this tale.

Another of the traditions instigated by Berrill was a monthly dinner in London, at which members would meet to eat and enjoy lively conversation. However, numbers dwindled, and by 1950 there were a mere four diners at the feast.

Doctor L. L. Ware allowed his membership to lapse; happily, however, he rejoined and, to this day, is still an active member, carrying the title '*fons et origo*' – founder and originator.

In the depressing year of 1950 Victor became the society's unofficial recorder, scribe and herald, taking on the onerous task of increasing the membership. With the entire Mensa pouch at his disposal – containing the princely sum of £25 – he placed notices in the more serious journals of the day. At the turn of 1959 a new communication spread its message – the *Mensa Correspondent*. In that same year Berrill's dream of 600 members was realised. It was also the year in which he attended his last Mensa meeting.

Groups were springing up all over the country, and the word spread to America. An American chronicler, who passed some time at the Society while on a journey to Britain, described his experience when he returned to the USA. A medical scribe, Peter A. Sturgeon, read the letter with interest and requested a test. He was successful and received authorisation to form a regional group, which was to become the foundation of American Mensa.

Shortly after this time, a lady took her place in American Mensa. Beloved and respected by all that knew her, Margot Seitleman, who, if not the queen of American Mensa, was assuredly its mother. Faithfully and loyally she served this, the largest Mensa, with devotion and love for thirty years, and is remembered with the highest affection by all her friends.

A letter arrived from Australia, where membership of the fast-spreading society was being sought. From this time forward the society flourished and, under the watchful eye of Victor Serebriakoff, spread to all corners of the globe. Today, more than 100 countries have members, and in a book entitled *Mensa, the Society for the Highly Intelligent*, written by Victor, and American Mensa's *A History of Mensa*, it is possible to read about the events and people of this society. Roland Berrill's aim of a membership of 600 was once a wild dream. World membership is now well over the 100,000-mark.

CHAPTER 3

The Ruby Anniversary

Mensa's Ruby Anniversary celebrations were purely social. Mensa was founded in October 1946 so there are no prizes for working out the year of the ruby celebrations. There were no lectures or seminars, no brain-stretching competitions or quizzes, just a gathering of members from far and wide celebrating forty years of this cosmopolitan society.

When the first draft of this chapter in Mensa's history was sent to the editor, he noted that he found it odd that forty years of cerebral achievement should be celebrated with none of the intelligent discussions or debates that had become the hallmarks of the society, and asked what the reason was. The only reason I can suggest is, that after forty years of such elevated intellectual pastimes, the members needed some time off from their mental exertions.

The first function of the weekend was the icebreaker, held at the National Liberal Club in London; it enabled members to meet visitors and the delegates of the International Board of Directors, whose meeting was convening in London prior to the great event. The onerous task of registering the guests fell to David Lally. He bravely refused help and the line of members and their guests grew longer and longer, winding its way down the staircase, through the hall and stopping just short of the front door and the street. Mensans do not wait patiently. The system was questioned, solutions offered, identities exchanged and, in the twinkling of an eye, total chaos reigned, turning a boring wait into a lot of fun for everyone – except David Lally. The proceedings got off to an auspicious start.

At this stage it would be a good idea if I introduced you to 'energy man' Lally. There are many of us in Mensa who are convinced that when he goes to bed at night he links into an enormous battery charger which energises him for the following day. Known to have attended four Mensa Christmas dinners, hundreds of miles apart, in three days, he is avoided at all costs by those low in blood sugar.

The following two days offered, amongst other things, a tour of St Paul's Cathedral, a City of London treasure hunt and a Chinese banquet. Having visited London many times in the past, and as David was ensconced in meetings, I decided that I would do something I had always wanted to do – just wander around the City of London and visit its well-known institutions including the much criticised Lloyd's building.

The banquet introduced many to a Mensa sport: namely, seeing how many Mensans can be squashed into one taxi. Answer, too many. It is surprising how many cab drivers throughout the Mensa world are still in possession of their licences.

Maurice Salzedo, a member of London Mensa, was one of the organisers of the Chinese meal. There were places for seventy people and, at the icebreaker, several people who had not previously booked approached him to request places. At the time Maurice had been helping friends to polish off three bottles of 'plonk' and had had a happy evening. Next morning he was not such a happy soul; he remembered the extra bookings he had taken and, opening his notebook, discovered that it was full of illegible and indecipherable hieroglyphs. He spent half of his day contacting people he thought might have paid him. To add to the confusion, David Lally had also accepted his share of eager beavers wishing to join in and their combined efforts resulted in eighty-one people turning up to claim the seventy places available. The obliging restaurant owners hurriedly carved more chopsticks and added tables in the hallway.

A Mensa team competing in *The Sunday Times* fun run in Hyde Park hoped members would go along to support them; they did, but not as hoped in droves; however, respectable support was on hand. A tour of Richmond was an attractive alternative particularly to the many foreign visitors, who welcomed the opportunity to see this very beautiful area. As one French lady said, 'It made my journey a plaisir to see zee watery England.'

Although the ten-day celebrations were to be spread throughout England, Scotland and Wales, it was no accident that the chosen venue for the Ruby Anniversary was Oxford, Mensa's birthplace. At 12 Saint John Street, Oxford, there is a circular yellow plaque erected on the wall of the house which reads: 'The International Society Mensa began here 1 October 1946.'

Wadham College was to be our home for three days. Nicholas Wadham died in 1609 and left his fortune to endow a college at Oxford. His widow, then aged seventy-five, took on the mammoth task of establishing the college, which was for men only. No women were to be employed in the college with the exception of a laundress, and she had to be 'of an age, condition, and reputation as to be above suspicion'. The female students of today must find that a quaint regulation.

The entrance to the college is in a quiet tree-lined street. The arched entrance contains the porters' lodge which opens on to the front quadrangle, in the centre of which is a perfectly mown lawn encased by a metal strip, past which no blade of grass dares to stray. An American visitor, avid for details of the college, laughed hysterically on learning that the lawn was a recent addition and had been created in 1809. 'Last year is recent,' she burbled. I told her of the popular theory as to why the grass in Ireland is so green. It is because all the Irish are in England walking on theirs!

The stonework of the beautiful old buildings, which had been restored in the late 1950s, glowed honey-coloured in the autumn sunshine. There are many famous names associated with Wadham College: Christopher Wren, Robert Blake (Cromwell's admiral), Cecil Day Lewis, C. B. Fry, the great sportsman, Thomas Beecham and Michael Foot.

The college boasts no lifts or *en-suite* bathrooms; no coffee shop or (heaven forbid) gift shop disturb its austere beauty. David and I contemplated the easiest way to haul our two heavy suitcases up the three narrow flights of stairs to our room. As in all good stories, a knight in shining mohair came to our rescue in the guise of Les Elmatton. A gentle giant of a man, he was accompanying his fiancée, Catherine Ford, the President of Canadian Mensa. As he picked up the bags they appeared to be filled with feathers rather than the raincoats, heavy sweaters and all-weather clothes with which they were packed before leaving home. He deposited them in our room with a big smile and we puffed along behind him. A large living room, sparsely furnished and devoid of all personal belongings, gave no clues as to its former student occupants. Leading from this were two narrow, single-bedded rooms, separated by a thin partition, which later gave rise to much amused tapping and signalling. Doors banging, people laughing and calling to each other reminded me of boarding school, this time without the strictures.

The second icebreaker heralded the official start to the Oxford section of the anniversary gathering. As we made our way to dinner, which was served in the hall of the College, I recognised people who had been in Dublin for the International Board of Directors meeting, members whom we had met at previous gatherings, and David introduced me to people who, until then, had just been voices on the telephone. In many instances I found that with my usual habit of imagining the faces belonging to the voices I had been wrong again.

The atmosphere was crackling with enthusiasm, bonhomie and excitement. Portraits of past scholars looked down on the chattering occupants of the long refectory tables. The length of the tables precluded conversation with anyone other than those in immediate earshot. I sat at the end of our table, with David on my left (deep in conversation with a fellow committee member), and was entertained by two ladies from the United States. They had met once at a dinner party given by mutual friends and, unfortunately, within a very few months they had both been widowed. Their friends, knowing that they shared a lot of common interests, encouraged them to spend some time together. They had done so and in the ensuing months they had become good friends. Having a considerable amount of free time, they volunteered to do some charity work and it was during this time that one of their co-workers joined Mensa. She had explained what the Society was all about and the two ladies, as is the norm, shuddered at the thought of trying the test even for fun. Her suggestion that they should at least know their IQs, made them succumb to the temptation and, like many brave people before them, they did the test.

Talking and laughing they recalled the day the results had arrived. Each one, totally staggered, had spent twenty minutes trying to reach the other on the phone. Finally giving up they had both replaced the receivers and a further frustrating half hour passed before they could share their news. Then came the moment all but the most gregarious Mensans dread, the first meeting. Sporting 'first time' buttons and clinging to each other for support, they went to the meeting. (The buttons are sometimes worn to enable hosts of events to recognise and welcome newcomers and introduce them to other members.) The meeting on this occasion was an 'eating meeting'. They were greeted by the group sitting at a large table and said that, within minutes, they were made to feel at ease. 'Mensa changed our lives,' said one of the ladies (I had better come clean at this stage and admit that I cannot remember their names). 'This is our first trip abroad and most certainly will not be our last,' they assured their small audience. Their families, whilst delighted for them, realised they had lost terrific baby-sitters to these new-found activities. Their excitement and animation were infectious and those listening to their story smiled and wished them a happy holiday.

Next morning we breakfasted in hall, which we learnt was one of the largest in Oxford. As we buttered and marmaladed, a young Swedish girl joined the table. She was travelling all over Europe compiling material for a travel book for students on limited budgets. Someone asked what she felt were the pitfalls of travelling alone and she revealed she had had no major problems as yet except possibly loneliness at times but, being multi-lingual, she was able to communicate with the people in most of the countries she was researching and she had found people very helpful.

She had arranged to meet an old school friend in Amsterdam and, sitting in the lounge of the hotel where they were to have lunch, she noticed some papers and a couple of magazines discarded on a table beside her; a familiar emblem caught her eye, the long-legged Mensa 'M'. She picked up the magazine and discovered it was an edition of the American *Bulletin*, the magazine distributed to all US Mensa members. As she had been away from home for some time she had not known of the ruby anniversary gathering. She had been scheduled to go to London, but altered her plans and headed for Oxford instead. Her adventures at this stage were interrupted by announcements of the day's events: a coach tour to Blenheim Palace, Stratford-upon-Avon and, finally, Warwick Castle.

Whilst sitting on a stone window sill waiting for the coach I had a talk with a delightful lady, Darlene Criss, from Kansas. She and her husband Jim had six children and, in addition, fostered twin boys, whom they regarded as their own children. She entered college for the first time at the age of forty and graduated five years later, then taking what she described as her 'first job' – teaching school. Having obtained a first degree, she spent a further two-and-a-half years completing her Master's degree in Education. Her thesis title reflects what she preached – it was 'Creativity'. Known affectionately from Wichita to Warsaw as 'head cluck', Darlene, through her devotion to Mensa, has won the admiration of many people. We were joined by Ken Loewen, described by Darlene as 'one o' mine'. This friendly and charming young man was enjoying his visit to Britain and to Oxford; he regaled us with an account of a missing tuxedo, promised but not ready when he left the States, which was to have been expressed to him at the college and had not as yet appeared. What had appeared, however, were the coaches to take us on our journey through the picturesque Oxfordshire countryside and to our first port of call, Blenheim Palace.

As we entered Woodstock Park, the landscape was shrouded in heavy mist and we were deprived of a view of the famous gardens, designed by Capability Brown. They were playing hide and seek; puffs of breeze momentarily revealed a tempting glimpse of their statuary and water gardens and then grey, swirling mists closed in once more. Superman Lally was waiting for us at the entrance with long, long strings of tickets streaming from his hands in the chill wind.

We entered the magnificent central hall with its dizzyingly high painted ceiling. One of the Duchesses of Marlborough had owned 120 spaniels which had been allowed to run riot in this hall, but fortunately both she and her dogs had long since departed. Our guide led us through the rooms at a respectable pace, checking carefully before closing each door that all her flock were together. It is a pity, but understandable, that visitors may no longer wander slowly through great houses at their own pace admiring their treasures as they used to be able to do. You miss many interesting details, especially if you are not tall or find yourself elbowed to the back of a group.

Having left the building one member of our party, who had obviously paid full attention to the gentle art of guiding, announced the departure of his tour. A guide book in one hand and an umbrella in the other, he gave us his impression of a whirlwind tour as he led the group through the gardens, now perfectly visible as the autumn sun had burned away the mists.

He pointed out the magnificent Grindling Gibbons stone carvings by the water gardens entitled 'Trophies of war'. They had cost the princely sum of forty pounds! With a deadpan expression and his glasses perilously low on his nose, our guide instructed us not to dawdle. We followed obediently, well, as obediently as Mensans ever do, and we approached to admire the fountain in the centre of the lake. 'This ...' he announced, but got no further. With a flourish he pointed the umbrella towards the spouting spray but it flew out of his hand and landed with a splash in the water. No arm rose out of the water brandishing the 'gamp' Excalibur-like, so we left him to fish out the offending article himself. The vast rolling lawns were frightening by virtue of their size and gave new meaning to the expression, 'mown and grown'.

The coaches took us through the grounds to the main road. We passed a snake of black limousines; Japanese faces peered out of the windows with the obligatory cameras firmly attached to one side of each face.

We were fully entertained on the next section of the journey by an elegant, grey-haired Texan, Judge Fite. With honey-coloured saddle bags thrown over his shoulder and wearing a cream stetson and immaculate apparel, he appeared very elegant – which is more than could have been said for several of us who had received a soaking from the wet sleeve of our erstwhile garden guide while he was fishing his umbrella out of the lake. Judge Fite announced without modesty that the forthcoming American Mensa annual gathering, 'La Republica de Tejas', to be held in Dallas the following July, would be the best ever, the biggest ever and have the most varied events ever. This was confirmed and enlarged upon by other members from the area who were travelling on the coach and the microphone was in almost constant use all the way to Stratford-upon-Avon. Listening to the good-humoured publicity I wondered how many of the cosmopolitan passengers on the bus would attend the gathering, never dreaming at the time that we would find ourselves there.

A banquet at Warwick Castle was arranged for the evening. Not wanting to spend more time on a coach we decided not to attend. Several people feeling likewise, opted to eat locally. Meeting later we discussed the options and being in the heart of England our choice was, naturally, a Chinese restaurant. After a very pleasant meal we made our way to one of the well-known Oxford pubs, the King's Arms, which was near the college and, enjoying a nightcap, encountered the first of the students returning for the Michaelmas term. Tables for two or three held seven or eight, and the small room was filled with laughter and noise. Closing time came all too soon, and back at the college we met the returning revellers from Warwick Castle.

One enthusiastic diner who had attended the medieval feast was Lorraine Boyce, a long-serving member of British Mensa, and she gave us a vivid description of the evening. The streets leading to the castle were quiet and peaceful in the dusk and, she said, it was not difficult to picture life as it must have been in medieval times. As she was making her way towards the dungeons, which have been refurbished for banqueting, she was joined by a young man from Germany whom she had not noticed on the coach. He confided to her that he had been at the castle earlier in the day and, having a romantic nature, had hidden inside the castle at closing time. Later, he had wandered around the grounds imagining himself back in ancient times and enjoying the experience of being 'king of the castle' for a few hours.

The guests sat down at the long tables and awaited the arrival of the great chafing dishes. But, it was decreed that, due to ye war being fought on foreign soil, the repast would be but a simple one of broth and bread. The sad faces of the serving wenches confirmed this news. A jester-cum-food-taster was appointed – none other than our own, David du Lally. As the sympathetic but disconsolate diners supped their broth and bemoaned the plight of the absent knights, a figure rushed into the room and proclaimed that the war had ended and that our knights had been victorious. Miraculously a feast appeared. Wine replaced water and shouts of the medieval toast 'wassail' echoed round the noisy dungeon. Beaming smiles lit the previously dejected faces of the serving girls and all present celebrated the successful outcome of the battle.

Wednesday, 1 October 1986, Mensa's fortieth birthday, was our last day in Oxford. After breakfast David had a brief meeting with some of the members of the International Board. I wandered into the fabled gardens in the 'back quad' of the college to have a look at the well-documented plants and trees. It occurred to me that it would be a nice gesture to present a tree to the college in commemoration of the anniversary celebrations. The following morning I suggested the idea to Dr Lance Ware, who was in full agreement and said that he would give some thought as to which type of tree would be most suitable. Some time later we read in the *Mensa Magazine* that a Canadian maple tree had been chosen. The International Chairman at that time, Hyman Brock, was Canadian, and the leaves of the tree turn a ruby red in October, the month of Mensa's founding – an appropriate choice. Unfortunately, the tree died as the soil was unsuitable, but the college has now replaced it with a tree which, they report, is flourishing. For garden lovers, it is *Eucommia ulmoides*, discovered by an Irishman, Dr Henry. It is of Chinese origin, prized for its bark which is sometimes used by the Chinese as a tonic, and it also yields an inferior quality latex. So ends your gardening lesson for today!

We wanted to visit the Bodleian Library and some of the illustrious colleges, so set off on our explorations. Passing through the entrance arch we glanced into the porters' lodge where Ken Loewen was in earnest conversation with the porters, obviously about his missing parcel. We made our way along the High and found Oriel College (I know it wasn't lost) and University College, Oxford's oldest college. At each corner we turned we came across a distinguished seat of learning. Unfortunately, many of the colleges were not open to visitors, and those that were, afforded a much restricted view of the grounds and only the exteriors of the buildings.

At one of the local hostelries we ran into other Mensans whom we joined for a morning drink. Drinking? In the morning? Permit me to explain. There were no communal meeting rooms provided at the college and, apart from the set meals, no refreshments were available either. So, needs must, we frequented the various pubs and coffee shops throughout the town. At this particular hour of the day the strongest drink required was black coffee.

Being aware of the vast numbers of books received by the Bodleian, we expected it would be a huge cavernous building of many floors. It was, in fact, quite small and very few of the five-and-a-half million volumes in its possession were in evidence; they are housed in seven buildings in different parts of Oxford. It is a legal deposit library which entitles it to claim a copy of every book published in Great Britain and Ireland. Duke Humfrey's library, dating back to 1488, was the original library on the site of the 'new' library which has been open only since 1602. Shortage of money prevented Duke Humfrey from buying printed books and, after endowing the library with his manuscripts, he was forced to close the doors about 1550 – even in those days recession reared its ugly head. Thomas Bodley opened the Bodleian Library and it was his far-sighted policy of collecting on a world-scale that has given Oxford its pre-eminence in Oriental manuscripts and many of its important holdings in all fields of scholarship.

We met other Mensans at the Library and decided to transform our thirst for knowledge into hunger for food. Like Topsy, our group just growed. More and more tables became filled with our strolling members and the poor waitresses were kept busy with the ever-increasing orders. Mensans are well used to the orderly chaos they create, as tables expand wherever and whenever they meet. Many a waiter and waitress around the globe must still be reeling after one of our visits. After lunch several of us meandered through the town. We all learned very quickly to dodge the bicycles which seemed to appear from nowhere; the sharp corners hid the cyclists from view until the last moment. Did they mentally chalk up a score as the pedestrians jumped for safety? One for a scare, two for a hit, perhaps? Passing Oxford's famed book shop, Blackwells, we popped in for a minute or two. An hour-and-a-half later we emerged, laden with parcels and leaving several of the others still browsing.

We were dressing for the banquet when there was a knock on our door and there stood the chairman of American Mensa, Amy Shaughnessy, with a plastic shampoo bottle clutched in her hand. Thinking she was having some difficulty washing her hair, naturally we invited her in. My guesswork was incorrect; the bottle contained vodka martini and she had come down to offer us a pre-party drink! Sharing glasses and the drink we admired her ingenuity.

The hall appeared very different that night, with the great hammer-beam roof and Jacobean screen casting their shadows in the candle-lit room. Sitting at high table I wondered (I seemed to do a lot of wondering that week) what Dr Ware and Victor Serebriakoff, further along the table, were thinking. Dr Lionel Lancelot Ware was, as you will recall, one of the two founders of Mensa and Victor Serebriakoff, Honorary President and often referred to as 'the father of Mensa', is the man who picked up the ball and ran with it when Mensa seemed about to falter in the 1950s. Could they have envisaged an occasion such as this? Did they think the society would last forty years? Could they, in their wildest dreams, have imagined there would one day be 100,000 members?

I looked at the people seated at the long tables; how many faces had become familiar to me in the few short years that I had been a member! One, which was not familiar at the time, belonged to Barry Grossman. He was to spend over a week in our home some years later – through the medium of the television. Barry was on *Countdown*, a well-devised and difficult quiz programme on which competitors have to solve anagrams and mathematical posers. He appeared as challenger for the requisite number of times, and went on to become the overall winner.

Sitting amongst an animated group was Ken Loewen – smartly dressed in the missing tuxedo? No, in a navy-blue suit. Seated between myself and Margaret Kavanagh, then treasurer of International Mensa, was the youngest member present, Lucas De Witt Sawyer, fourteen years old, from the United States. He was accompanied by his mother and grandmother – three generations of Mensans. He was at the time rather shy and Margaret and I did our best to draw him into the conversation. Due to business pressures Margaret has unfortunately had to withdraw from her committee work and we miss her company at the various gatherings. Also at the table was Marcia Dwyer, who had travelled the furthest distance – from New Zealand. In all, there were about twenty countries represented that night, including a very large contingent from the United States.

The guest of honour and speaker was Professor Richard Gregory, head of brain research and Professor of Neuropsychology at Bristol University. He spoke interestingly about a snooker-playing robot. With a TV eye it could differentiate between the colours of the snooker balls, correct mistakes and plan strategy. One newspaper reporting the event acidly commented that the robot was nothing new, Steve Davis (recent world champion) had been around for years!

It had been hoped that a member of the royal family would attend the dinner, although we did not know which one of them it might be. Each visitor to the dinner had to supply a photograph and background details when applying for their invitation to attend. Speculation was rife as the applications came in. Princess Diana undoubtedly topped the popularity poll. None of us expected it to be Her Majesty the Queen but all agreed that the Duke of Edinburgh was a more likely choice. Prince Charles was a definite possibility, Prince Andrew was away, Princess Anne would be an able family representative.

The guesswork ran riot until the long-awaited letter from Buckingham Palace finally arrived. 'We very much regret due to the pressure of other commitments we are unable ...' Disappointment reigned, along with the royal family! Now may be an appropriate time to invite them to celebrate Mensa's Golden Anniversary in 1996.

After the dinner goodbyes were said and addresses exchanged. Those of us staying at Wadham College returned to a small bar in use that evening, but after a short time the shutters came down. A quick word and, I suspect, a few pounds from our knight errant, Les Elmatton, and the bar miraculously reopened; the evening continued until ... late!

We had been away for a week and the next morning we were part of the home-bound. Darlene and Ken came to see us off. We had enjoyed their company and had a lot of fun together. As we waited for our transport the returning students mingled with departing Mensans. Bicycles added to the clutter of baggage in the entrance, students popped into the porters' lodge to collect their mail and to seek information. It was with real regret that we left the college for the last time; we felt we had been truly educated at Oxford.

CHAPTER 4

Doing it by the book

Some Mensans are by choice 'magazine-Mensans'; they do not attend meetings, either locally or nationally, and are content for their only contact with the society to be through the pages of their national magazine, the regional newsletter (where available) or the journals of the special interest group to which they have chosen to belong.

The monthly *Mensa Magazine* is received by all British and Irish members and a considerable number of Mensans living abroad. Its contributors are mainly Mensa members but, occasionally, outside writers can be found within its covers.

Until fairly recently it would not be truthful to say that I waited on the doorstep for its arrival. I found it too technologically and scientifically slanted and used to browse through its pages rather than read it thoroughly. However, help was at hand in the form of a 'new-look' publication and I now look forward to a really good read.

A diary section gives updates on Mensa happenings, the articles are topical, varied and interesting. For example, there have been features on real tennis, which is enjoying a strong renaissance; the Chippendales, male strippers who are currently in vogue; the preparation of a gossip column, which presumably enjoys snippets from other people's lives; a day at a Mills & Boon workshop; photography; manufacturing board games; Mensa's bionic woman (thanks to cosmetic surgery); an IQ test for dogs; and one woman's experience of hypnotic regression. Technology is a regular feature, profiles of members and non-members give an insight into careers and occupations which make fascinating reading. John McNulty writes his monthly technological and scientific column with brevity and wit and his jottings often provide food for argument in subsequent editions. Several pages of readers' letters cover a wide range of topics. Mark Griffin, the Special Interest Groups officer, reports on newly-proposed groups and information concerning the existing ones. These Special Interest Groups are a very important part of Mensa and often snippets and reports about them encourage people to spread their wings a little and join them.

One of the most enjoyable and frustrating features in each edition is the page of brain teasers, edited by Ken Russell. Ken is the compiler of many British Mensa-approved puzzle books, several of which were co-written with Philip Carter. They jointly edit the newsletter of the Enigma Special Interest Group and a monthly puzzle magazine. Skipping daintily past the more complicated mathematical puzzles, I do succumb every now and then to the brain-stretching numerical conundrums (in order to see if they really are as tantalising as I had imagined and, yes, they are). The word-twisters and puzzles are challenging time-guzzlers. According to Ken there is a very good response to the Brain Teaser page, anything between twenty to a hundred replies each month. 'Kickself' is the heading for the lateral-thinking teasers in each issue and, whether one has reached the solution or not, it makes me want to do just that.

Kickself made its debut at an international meeting in the early 1980s when, chatting with Isaac Asimov (a Mensa member of long standing),

Victor Serebriakoff and Clive Sinclair were asked, 'What was the first artefact made by man that broke the sound barrier?' The answer, 'the tip of a whip', was given, Ken said, by Clive.

The editor of *Mensa Magazine*, Simon Clark, says, 'If people feel they have an interesting article, feature, essay or letter to contribute, they should give me a call. A short phone call will often help clarify the suitability, subject matter and length, and is much more personal than a letter. We are always interested in receiving good and professional material and every submission received is carefully read.' Like Mr Delmonte Simon is a man who likes to say yes.

Ten or more pages carry announcements of local and regional meetings and provide a valuable guide to members travelling outside their own area. The 'classifieds' are extremely diverse, ranging from general business advertising to services, and from personal advertising from Mensans who wish to find others of like mind to situations wanted and vacant. The covers of the magazine are magnificently produced in full colour and the standard is consistently high.

Simon works under the auspices of the editorial board of the British Mensa Committee. When I asked him for a profile of himself, all that my cajoling and pleading elicited was the information that Simon Clark is the editor of *Mensa Magazine*. He did, however, readily answer my numerous questions, disguised as research.

'Where does the material used in its articles and features originate?'

'Mostly from members. Some, but very few, outside contributors do write from time to time but, obviously, we prefer to use articles sent by members.'

'Do you find it difficult to refuse material?' (I had an ulterior motive here; I was thinking of the half-written article hidden amongst my non-compatible discs.)

'Yes.' His reply was very positive. 'It is the hardest thing in the world to inform people that their pride and joy is not suitable for this particular publication.'

'How can members know what is acceptable or not?' (Sneaky.)

Kent Van Cleave became the editor of *Mensa Bulletin* in 1985; he started out as a volunteer, but when American Mensa decided to make the editorship a paid position he became the first professional editor.

Not one to leave things alone, he set about redesigning the magazine from cover to cover. Technology played a big part in making life easier in the ensuing years as computer sophistication aided the production. Today much of the material is submitted either on diskettes or by electronic mail.

The *Mensa Bulletin* is the publication enjoyed by over 55,000 American Mensans – and me. Kent Van Cleave, the editor, says that the most popular section is 'Letters to the editor', probably because it provides the most highly concentrated grist for the reader's mental mill. 'The 2% solution' offers members' solutions to questions posed in previous issues (mostly concerning world problems). Reports of local groups, gatherings and Special Interest Groups are regular features. 'Word play' is one of my own favourite pages (subjecting the English language to good-natured abuse is the official definition of this most entertaining regular feature). It is rescued by 'SOTS', the Save Our Tongue Society, which decries the misuse of the English language. All manner of shoddy thinking, advertising and deceptive rhetoric are dealt with in the bulletin's regular 'exposé' column. The book reviews are of particular interest as they provide an excellent opportunity to learn what people in the US are reading and writing.

One aspect of Mensa that Kent particularly enjoys is the ever-present humour and, in particular, punning. Following a fishing trip, Kent was exposed to remarks such as, 'Did you go with Ray?' He replied, 'No. I went with a grouper other guys.' Others followed: 'I am waiting with baited breath.' 'Aw, don't be shellfish,' and so on. I regret that there is no plaice in my book for any more of those lines.

Two of Kent's greatest interests are music (sad for a man who is hard of herring) and philosophy. Music has played an important part in his life and, at one stage, was a full-time occupation. He spent three years playing in US Army bands and then acquired 'the world's most practical degree: a Bachelor of Music in Theory'.

Philosophy plays an equally important role in his life; his self-published booklet, *Evolutionary Foundations for Philosophy,* stressed evolutionary themes. He reads everything within reach but has a preference for good science fiction, theoretical physics (my favourite, of course), cosmology, Jungian personality typology, anthropology, palaeontology, neuropsychology and, presumably, just about every other known 'ology'.

One copy of the Bulletin proudly displayed on its back cover the names of seventy-one recipients of the MERF (Mensa Education and Research Foundation) scholarship awards. It must be as rewarding for all the truly dedicated American Mensa workers as it is for the delighted award winners. The enormous support for this cause is ever present in all the journals and newsletters in the US. The awards are not confined to Mensans and a subsequent copy of the Bulletin had short and delighted acknowledgements of appreciation from some of the beneficiaries.

One of the recent covers featured a photograph of thirty-one members of American Mensa – travellers to the People's Republic of China. The story of their journey, related by Karen Koezier, made fascinating reading. They visited the Great Wall and the Forbidden City, and were astounded at the size of the latter (9,999 rooms spread over 250 acres). One elderly lady from southern China, hobbling along on tiny bound feet, told them that for her the visit fulfilled an almost impossible childhood dream. They left the cities in order to explore rural areas and revel in the 'real' China, and the reader was left in no doubt as to the enjoyment and success of their adventure.

Mindful of the aims of Mensa – to foster intelligence – the Bulletin is a wide-ranging journal of entertainment, humour, informed opinion and intelligent discussion and argument.

MC^2 is the publication of Canadian Mensa. Gatherings and reports are printed in French and English but the majority of the articles are in English. Devilish puzzles by K. H. (Wicks) Wickremasinghe, and Rosalie Moscovitch provide hair-tearing entertainment and, as in all of the national journals, there are many informative and informed articles along with the *International Journal*, which is bound in with all national magazines.

Irene Renata Radek's column, 'In the spotlight', discusses film, television and entertainment. 'Think twice', co-written by the Rev. Richard Rose and Peter R. Smith, addresses all aspects of subjects such as 'Jesus – who was He?' and abortion. Local issues are debated and, of course, the letters pages, as with all of Mensa's publications, are lively. The cartoons amongst its pages always raise a smile and, in common with all the other national Mensa journals and magazines, it is never dull.

Each national Mensa publishes its own magazine in the language of the country, and all discuss world issues and subjects pertinent to their own particular country.

The Mensa Yearbook, published annually by Mensa Publications Ltd in Britain and edited by Robert Allen, has provided me with invaluable contact with members and a tremendous amount of amusing reading. Approximately one-tenth of the members (trust me – I counted them) responded to the opportunity to present a mini-profile of themselves in twenty words or fewer. There are members who are as sweet as Sugar and Spice, daring as Swash and Buckle, investigative as Holmes and Watson; there are Shakespearian followers, Hamlet and McBeth; weights and measures controllers, Bushel and Peck; law and order men, Sergeant and Constable and, all in good taste, Salt and Pepper. There is a Bishop but, alas, no Actress.

Equally varied are people's interests. Computers, reading and cats appear in every column on every page, but there are more unusual hobbies too. One man describes himself as an amateur gynaecologist, another sees himself as a run-of-the-mill accountant and part-time brain surgeon. For me the most intriguing entry is that of the member who wishes to avoid all contact with other Mensans. I telephoned and explained my mission. 'May I ask you why you want to avoid contact with other Mensans?' I enquired. 'No, you may not,' was his reply as he hastily replaced the receiver. That, I must admit, put a silly grin on my face for days.

Science fiction, writing, games and puzzles, music, theatre, cars and sport feature largely. Two golfers were interested in meeting other players, and I hope that they fare better than one poor Mensan, who, whilst on a business trip to a remote country, opted to play a lone round of golf in a very dangerous area. The committee of the club would not permit him to venture out alone and insisted that he take a caddie. Reluctantly the Mensan agreed and, as the two men approached the first tee, he noticed that the caddie carried not only a bag of clubs but a bag of assorted guns as well.

All went well for three holes, then a ball was hit into the rough and the searching player was brought to a frozen halt as a massive, poisonous snake approached him. The caddie instructed him to remain absolutely still and, taking a gun from the bag, with one clean shot killed the snake. Shaking but determined to carry on, they proceeded without incident until they reached the seventh fairway where a mis-hit ball flew into a large clump of trees. Making his way towards the miniature forest the golfer began to search with his club. A growling sound announced the presence of a large animal and, without further warning, a tiger sprang towards the unfortunate man. Quick as a flash the caddie took a large rifle from the bag and the leaping animal was stopped in midair. Sheer bravado and courage kept the shaking man 'on course'. By the time he had reached the tenth hole he had recovered enough to enjoy the peace and quiet and was hitting the ball quite well. The ball was sitting nicely on a little mound by the river. Reaching for an iron from his bag he addressed the ball and was preparing to hit what he was determined would be a magnificent shot when a large crocodile, with tears in its eyes, slithered out from behind him with teeth bared, headed straight for him. As the creature grabbed his ankle he screamed at the caddie, who was just standing by quietly and doing absolutely nothing to help him. The golfer beat the crocodile with his club until it finally released him and disappeared into the water. He turned on the caddie and roared at him, 'Why did you not shoot it, you could see what it was doing to me?' 'Sorry, sir, I couldn't help you this time,' replied the caddie to the infuriated golfer, 'I'm afraid you don't get a shot at this hole.' (Not really true but the story will please animal lovers and golf haters.)

British Mensa is divided into twelve regions, each of which has its own monthly newsletter containing information about local events and meetings; articles, poetry and general reports. These publications are restricted to eight pages and only the size of print varies. Irish Mensa's *Impress* is edited by Eileen Gormley, who worked in computers and accountancy, and is a relatively recent Mensan. She complained some years ago to David that there was little Mensa information available in the Irish midlands. 'Write something,' said David. Eileen did, and her article was picked up by local newspapers, one of which particularly admired her style and asked her to submit another feature. This was duly published and she jettisoned numbers for words and embarked on a new career as a professional journalist. Twice daily she scrambles to meet her deadlines for the national newspapers.

Impress covers all Ireland, region number one, and its news, reviews, stories and crossword puzzle are entertaining. 'Pandora's crossword' is the brainchild of Elaine Kennedy (Elaine Good). Crosswords are not the only things that occupy Elaine's cryptic mind; she is also the SIGHT Officer for Irish Mensa, welcoming Mensans from other countries, finding accommodation, helping them with their problems and, of course, introducing them to local Mensans. This is a most important office in Mensa, assuring visitors of a welcome wherever they choose to stray. On occasion non-members have tried to avail themselves of the service, but usually without success as official identification is readily accessible throughout the world. Elaine's warm friendliness certainly helped to smooth my path in Irish Mensa and I know her work as SIGHT Officer has resulted in many happy vacations for members, who heap praise on her head for her kindness and ready smile.

I asked Elaine what prompted her to join Mensa. 'Mostly the need to prove I was not a vegetable.' Mother of two, Elaine includes Sarah and Conor in many Mensa outings, and these bright youngsters are well known to Irish Mensans. It was purely by accident that we recently discovered that she not only holds a degree in philosophy, but is also a scholar of Trinity College, Dublin.

The covers of *Impress* have for years been graced with the cartoons of John Lucas. Topical events, caricatures and tongue-in-the-cheek visual comment are the speciality of this quiet Mensan. It takes time to find his JAYEL signature cunningly hidden in the illustrations.

Bagpipe, Scrumpy, Empress, SEMantics, Trans-Pennine Express are some of the other monthly regional newsletters. Some are produced by special editors and others by the local secretaries themselves. Local Secretaries (LocSecs) are the bedrock of the society and it is an indisputable fact that without them Mensa would probably fall apart.

The first letter I received from just such a LocSec came from Ruth Ley, representing Wigan and Bolton. Ruth was born ten miles from where she now lives in Bolton. With great craftiness she suggested that if I wanted to know her age I should buy the yearbook and look it up.

Some of the queries Ruth receives are easily dealt with (Where is the next meeting?), others less so (My son has just passed his test, where is his certificate?). Nervous new members are given encouragement when attending meetings for the first time; Ruth can arrange transport for them, she chats with them and helps to break the ice. She also helps by suggesting suitable special interest groups or setting up contact with other members of similar interests.

She gets many enquiries from the parents of junior Mensans regarding schooling and puts them in touch with the relevant advisers. Her biggest grumble is early-morning telephone calls on Saturdays. She has now invested in an answering machine in order to preserve the sanctity of the Saturday morning lie-in.

Newsletters announce meetings or outings which may be planned three to six months in advance, and these can be a source of worry. 'OK,' said Ruth, 'so I organised a Chinese evening on Burns' night, nobody's perfect.'

Things can go wrong after an event has been advertised in *Mensa Magazine* or a regional newsletter. For instance, the venue for the Christmas dinner in Dublin was razed to the ground less than a week before the appointed date, and the LocSec, Paul McKinley, was faced with finding an alternative restaurant – everywhere was heavily booked in the two weeks preceding the holidays – and contacting members, some of whom are not available by telephone.

LocSecs are busy people, often with families and full-time jobs, and when events at times are badly attended it can be disheartening for them. Ruth considers herself fortunate in having a hard core of loyal supporters who turn out in rain, hail and snow, and even when there is a good programme on television. This makes it all worthwhile.

The *International Journal* appears ten times a year. A copy of each edition is included in all the national magazines and the journal is sent to all direct members of International Mensa. It provides isolated members with news, committee reports, short articles and book reviews. The book reviewer, David Gamon, is himself an author, specialising in biblical novels and he is also a journalist. He receives on average two books a week, mainly from Britain and the US. Now retired, he has time to read and enjoy the books and prefers not to speed read. 'Entre nous', the classified section of the *International Journal,* is an amazing melting pot of information-seeking. Researchers requiring data for books, those trying to trace family members in other countries, music lovers hoping to complete record collections, sick people seeking medical information from others similarly affected, those looking for out-of-print books, travellers eager for contact with natives of the countries they propose to visit, people wanting pen friends of other cultures and even those seeking irreplaceable lost recipes – all advertise in this useful column. Australia, New Zealand, Hong Kong, France, Italy, Hawaii, Great Britain, The United States, Spain, Colombia, the Philippines – the list of fact-searchers is truly cosmopolitan. The stamps of the letters received would, I am sure, make the basis of a very good collection.

Isolated M is undoubtedly a most affectionately regarded publication. This little green rag, as it is irreverently dubbed by its editorial team, is dispatched worldwide to all isolated members, Direct International Members and US citizens living and working abroad. It is also available to all members on subscription. It is in this area that the magazine has a power that subscriber journals all over the world would kill for. Hysterical would not be too strong a word to describe the letters from subscribers who have failed to notice that their subscription renewal date has passed. A red heart warns the reader of the penultimate copy and a red X announces the final number.

One recent letter, from a man named Dave, stated that he could not get through the year without his copies of the little green rag (LGR). Reading further, I discovered that this isolated Mensan was none other than Dave Felt, Chairman of American Mensa. Another writer began, 'Words cannot describe my distress, my subscription has run out.' What is the magic of this LGR? The answer can be found in its friendly, warm, chatty, funny, informative, groan-provoking pages, which link isolated and not-so-isolated members in one hundred countries throughout the world.

Dignified titles have no place on its editorial board. The editor, Darlene Criss, is the 'head cluck'. It was through years of reading this magazine that we became familiar with the various regular columnists, and we were delighted that one recent edition carried photographs of all the editorial board, with whose names we had become familiar. One face was that of Dr Sam Pobanz MD who writes a column entitled 'Sputterings'. My mind-picture of him had been a hundred per cent wrong. This tall and very slightly built man stood proudly with his fellow journalists sporting a tee-shirt which read, 'No I am not on steroids. But thank you for asking.' The 'Sputterings' page offers wise advice such as, 'When you take a chocolate bar to eat in the shower, remember the soap is white.' Its life-enhancing guidance includes remarks such as, 'If you want to live long enough to enjoy certain things in life, you have to give them up.' And here are a couple of its positive life-saving hints: 'Do not pick up a tree branch on which you are standing.' And 'Do not walk with a chain saw which is running.' Aside from these odd, amusing 'Sputterings' Sam Pobanz expresses serious views on, for example, the heartbreak caused by the unnecessary carnage on the roads, the plight of the world's underprivileged people, and on life in general.

The front page of the LGR, entitled 'The Spirit of Ms Criss', updates and informs her Mensan chicks all over the world. The Editorial Board are the proud owners of a large map which is dotted with coloured pins marking the towns and countries of the journal's devotees. Apart from being the first Vice Chairman of American Mensa, Darlene also represents her country both nationally and internationally so her knowledge of happenings within the Mensa world is first hand and is reported in her own witty and warm fashion in the ten editions which are produced annually.

Before and during the Gulf War many appreciative letters were received from members of the armed forces. *Isolated M* contributed much needed news, and it is quite common in peace time too to read communications in the 'Mensallany' pages from military personnel posted abroad. Interesting glimpses of different life styles and cultures are reported by its cosmopolitan followers.

A reference to Yvonne Mgadi in one edition of the LGR sent me running to my files. Yvonne, a member of British Mensa, had written to me and was anxious to make a contribution to this book. She had joined at the age of nineteen and her letter gave sound advice on how to approach the test. 'Get there early and smile at the supervisor,' she suggested. 'This gets rid of tensions.' That made sense. Yvonne is a member of the journalists' Special Interest Group and has written articles, and a novel which she is hoping will be published. She is unemployed at the moment, but has been accepted by the National Technical Institute for the Deaf at the Technical Institute of Technology in New York to study for a bachelor's degree in computer sciences. Yvonne has been deaf from birth and suffers from a degenerative eye disease, but she wants to encourage other sufferers not to give up. 'I feel that I can now achieve the impossible,' she writes. 'The sky's the limit, you know.'

The 'Feghootia' are sent to try us – and try us again. The success of these tales is measured by the volume of groans they provoke.

'By Request' is a column dedicated to bringing a little sunshine into the lives of people who, for one reason or another, are suffering from the downside of life. A card or a word of cheer can sometimes lift the dark clouds and members are invited to send the names of people who may be glad of a kind thought. Kind thoughts are typical of this little green rag.

For some Mensans these communications are not just informative and enjoyable reading, but also the means to an end – personal contact with others. On most nights of the year there will probably be a Mensa meeting somewhere in the world. A pub meeting once a month would appear to be the most popular form of gathering in British and Irish Mensa. Many people who do not drink are quite content with a soft beverage, lively conversation and the good company. There are also eating meetings, board-games nights, quizzes, bowling sessions, theatre and cinema visits, rambles, at homes, museum visits, lectures, musical evenings, treasure hunts, abseiling, mountain climbing, parties, ice skating – the list is almost endless. Off-beat ideas prove popular and, as one LocSec said, 'They bring the members out of the woodwork.' There has been an unusual tool and gadget evening, a 6.30 a.m. breakfast meeting for night workers, a culinary cruise and bungy jumping – the ideas just keep on and on.

CHAPTER 5

Letter from America

Many times over the years we had heard, read and been told of American Mensa's successful and enjoyable annual gatherings. The variety of events, coupled with the huge number of members who attended these gatherings, appeared to be the magic ingredients of their success. When an invitation to the Annual Gathering to be held in Dallas was extended to David, in his capacity as international chairman, he accepted it with pleasure. We decided to make it a part of our annual holiday, travelling to Canada and other parts of the United States after the gathering.

After a journey of twenty-four hours, plagued with delays, the announcement of our landing was a welcome sound and, as we stared through the windows of the plane into the inkiness of the night, a bowl of sparkling and brightly shining jewels lit the gloom – the lights of Dallas, at last.

Making our way along the airport concourse we were delighted to see a smiling girl holding up a Mensa emblem. She explained that Ken Loewen had hired a car to meet us, but, as the time passed and we had failed to appear, he had returned the car. Knowing that she and a friend were meeting another passenger at the time of our next possible flight, Ken had asked her to watch out for us. The gesture was greatly appreciated. There is nothing more disorienting than arriving jet-lagged at a strange airport at night. When the spirit of adventure was handed out I must have been in the ladies' room. We piled into her small car; the baggage was stowed under us, over us and around us, and with the tyres almost flattened, the five of us set off happily for our hotel on the outskirts of the town. In a short time we arrived all in one piece and, uncoiling ourselves, we retrieved our luggage, battered duty-free cigarettes, arms and legs, and checked in at the busy reception desk. Even in our dazed state we were pleased to see so many people we had met previously.

The committee had thoughtfully arranged an executive room for us which, in turn, allowed us the use of a courtesy suite. Next morning, presenting the printed invitation necessary to gain access, we discovered a large, comfortable room containing a buffet table laden with cereals, rolls and breads, fruit and all the ingredients essential for a busy time-rationed executive breakfast. Deeply padded chairs with conveniently placed low tables, writing desks stocked with scribbling pads, hotel stationery, and a television set with its sound turned low, provided an oasis of peace and tranquillity – disturbed only by the crunching of corn flakes. Through bleary eyes we watched the morning news: Colonel Oliver North, white-faced and serious, explaining the complications of Irangate.

Standing in line at the registration desk (see how quickly I dropped 'queueing'?), we met and talked to members from all over the US. I have no doubt our Irish Mensa badges were a contributory factor to the immediate friendliness we met with. I must confess that when I first encountered this system of people-labelling, it reminded me of crackling old newsreels featuring refugee children with their outsize and always crooked badges of identification, and their bewildered faces, watching and waiting to be claimed by strangers who were to become their instant families. Given the large numbers of people one encounters at meetings I rapidly changed my mind and found it an invaluable aid to my failing memory.

We collected our programmes (or 'programs' I suppose I should say, being in the USA) and waded through the contents. Having studied the enormous list of events due to take place at the weekend, we decided that we should use our only opportunity to see the city of Dallas before things became totally hectic. Our bemused cab driver, who presumably had never before been asked for a tour of the centre of Dallas, looked at us with pitying eyes and, shrugging his shoulders, set off towards the city.

The design inventiveness of the modernistic buildings – which at times appeared to defy gravity – would have pleased even Prince Charles. Rising from the ground at amazing angles they sheared off at the top and returned to earth at totally different angles. Windows of darkened glass added to the effect by reflecting and distorting the structures opposite them. It was almost surreal. We were suffering from the effects of too much coffee and too little sleep!

The most moving sight we saw on our excursion was, of course, the spot where President John F. Kennedy was shot. We told our now slightly-thawed guide that we had seen the late President when he had visited Ireland. He stared hard at us in his driving mirror and the light suddenly dawned. 'You folks foam Irelan'?' he astutely enquired. 'Yes,' we responded. 'Ahhhhh!' he breathed. That obviously explained everything. Silence followed, then, after a couple of minutes, 'Famine over yet?' he asked. With one eye on the passing landscape and the other on the driver, David explained patiently that it had ended a very long time ago. We continued our tour while he digested this information. 'You see,' he said, beginning in the middle of his sentence, 'my Granmammy tole me everyone was starving and that is why my family is Irish.' This, we gathered, was the son, of a son, of a son from Erin's green isle. 'You will be able to tell her all is well now,' said David with a twinkle in both eyes, now happily together again. 'Nope, she's gorn,' he replied, not qualifying where she had 'gorn' to. Not wanting to get further involved, we accepted the statement without question.

Having finally run out of places to show us and at a bit of a loss as to where to take us next, our driver ended the expedition at the doors of Nieman Marcus, saying, 'You all have a good visit mind'. As he prepared to enter the stream of traffic, we heard him singing at the top of his voice, through the open cab window, a totally off key rendering of 'Danny Boy'. Were we the first people to notice that Dallas is amazing?

We entered the cool and elegant world-famous store but, luckily for David, were unsuccessful in finding any of the mandatory family gifts and so we settled for lunch instead. Later, as we meandered along the streets, busy at this time of the day with smartly dressed and hurrying business people, the heat and jet lag caught up with us and, giving up our wanderings, we returned to the hotel.

Three hours' broken sleep the previous night had not done much for my maladjusted mental clock, so, leaving David chatting with acquaintances old and new, I sneaked back to the courtesy suite for a cup of coffee and settled into a chair to watch the continuing appearance of Colonel North, his questioning and responses. A gap in the proceedings followed as I fell asleep in the comfortable chair.

Darlene Criss invited us to be her guests at dinner on our first evening. By the time we crossed the complex to the restaurant, the heat of the day had given way to the pleasant and ever present breeze which wrapped us in its cocoon of warmth. We particularly appreciated this as our summer that year had consisted of cloud and rain, alternating with rain and cloud, the temperatures barely surpassing those of winter.

A Mexican restaurant was the venue and we were introduced to spicy and unusual varieties of food. An attentive host sitting at a table within earshot was regaling his guests with his encyclopaedic knowledge of the culture and food of Mexico. Not called 'radar ears' for nothing, I soaked up his dissertation and stored it in the memory bank to be aired at a future date. Tostadifas, he told his attentive guests, are tortillas crisply fried. I fancied some of those. Enchilados, he said, are tortillas stuffed and folded, covered with sauce and baked. I fancied them too, in fact I fancied everything he described. As I sipped a potent tequila sunrise, I continued to eavesdrop on how the Aztecs had introduced maize to the civilised world and a discourse on beans and peppers. My quest for knowledge at this stage was wearing a bit thin and I was relieved when the waiter approached to take the order. David gave me a funny look as I ordered with great authority.

A long table of assorted and animated Mensans added to the hubbub of the room. It was a lively and entertaining evening and it did not take us long to tap into the now accustomed friendliness of members and to join in the various conversations while our ears got used to the medley of accents. A man sitting opposite me hailed from Fort Worth in Texas, which he painstakingly taught me to pronounce correctly as 'Fot Wuth'. Having mastered this I filed it in my own meagre little mental file under the heading of 'Anne's Mensa education and research'. Before we returned to the hotel across the grassy complex some bright spark warned us to watch out for snakes. Have you ever seen anyone walk on air? Had you been with us, you would have done.

The lobby and hospitality rooms were thronged with people and it was here that I encountered the Mensa hug for the first time. Used by some members delighted to see old friends again, the hug is given only with permission. A girl I was speaking to, seeing my amusement, told me that some people find it embarrassing and do object, so approval is always sought. Refusal, she explained, was accepted without offence or comment. A couple of minutes later a very sweet lady, who had met David in St Louis, squeezed her way through the crowded room to ask my permission to give him a hug; she reappeared almost immediately to apologise for not giving me a hug too. After giving my permission, I too became one of the 'hugged'. I never caught her name in all the hulla-baloo, and when later I told David of the incident I was not in the least bit surprised to learn that he could not recall her name – he has diffi-culty with mine at times.

This inherited affliction has caused him great embarrassment in the past. Some years ago at a business exhibition he landed a large and very profitable order. Carefully recording the details he used his usual ploy of asking, 'Is that company or company ltd?' Most people would then state the full company name, thus saving his face. Writing furiously he heard the prospective buyer respond, 'Oh no! You tried that one last year, David. If you can't remember the name you won't be able to send the order, will you?' Without another word, and with a big grin on his face, he walked away. An efficient secretary did remember the firm and the order was dispatched.

Hugging is a very American Mensa phenomenon and, in the right surroundings and in the US it is pleasant and harmless (but not armless) fun for those who participate. A few years ago someone tried to introduce it into British Mensa where it died an instant death in face of the tight British reserve. We heard that there was a concealed competition going on throughout the Dallas gathering; apparently there were several judges who hugged and were hugged and who eventually met and decided upon the various merits or otherwise of the assorted huggers and huggees.

A 'get-acquainted matrix' was included in the registration package. This was a piece of paper divided into boxes, each of which contained a question. The idea was to get you to approach people and obtain a signed response. For instance, you had to find someone who had made a parachute jump, someone who was colour blind, someone who had read a Mills & Boon novel. This allowed even the shyest people to talk to others easily, and the searching caused much amusement. I am colour blind and I found myself in popular demand. Furthermore, I have two friends who write for Mills & Boon *and* I have read some of their books – my popularity boiled over.

There seemed to be an incredible number of people milling around the registration desk. A subsequent report in *A History of Mensa*, a concise, well-constructed and easily read booklet, published by American Mensa Ltd, placed the number attending the gathering at 1,322. In the interests of accuracy, I might add that I received a letter from the AG chairman, Carol Hilson, placing the total at 1,126. The lower figure probably refers to those who registered for the gathering and the higher figure to those who just visited for part of a day – either way, a lot of people. The well-produced 26-page programme was informative and inviting. The events were, to say the least, eclectic; every taste was catered for, and then some. Meeting rooms and hospitality suites, both smoking and non-smoking, occupied two floors. There were storage rooms for the vast quantity of food and drink and, for those of a reclusive nature, a 'quiet room' was provided; here no talking or smoking was permitted. If it was used I cannot say, as, being a chatterbox and a smoker, I did not visit this purified den of silence!

'Registration' is a system used at American Mensa gatherings. A fee covers all snack food and drink in the hospitality rooms and most of the entertainment and lectures. Those on a tight budget have a total package with no surprise expenses. Presumably it also saves the considerable amount of time and work involved in issuing individual tickets for each event. Formal lunches and banquets are charged for separately and, for those not liking the formality, or not wanting the expense, the hospitality suites with their snack provisions were open for twenty hours each day.

Carol and her committee performed daunting feats of organisation. They staffed the information desks, kept the bulletin boards updated, solved problems and generally helped in every way possible. Day and night her team replenished empty plates, refilled the huge bins with cold drinks and beer, and kept the heavy coffee urns topped up. All this, with good-natured cheerfulness, continued without ceasing for the duration of our stay. I was fascinated to see olives the size of plums, piles of wafer-thin slices of cheese which must have taken days to slice, a bewildering array of snack crackers and, most tempting of all, bowls of a marvellous spicy dip called salsa, for which, despite many attempts, I did not succeed in obtaining the recipe.

In aid of North Texas Mensa scholarship fund a 'pie-in-the-face' competition was held. For several months prior to the gathering members had been voting at twenty-five cents a time with as many votes as you wished to buy (sounds a bit like Ireland in the good old days when the slogan was, 'Vote early and often'), to decide which local member should receive the dubious honour of a pie in the face. On the evening that the winner (or loser, depending on which side of the pie you were) was announced, bids were made for the honour of throwing the pie. The room was crowded and the pace was brisk as the bids reached very high figures. Two enthusiastic bidders remained, one representing a group called the Bawdy Broads, the other, the present International Chairman, Velma Jeremiah. Egged on by the crowd, the bidding continued to rise steeply until calls for two pies were heard, and, after a brief consultation, the committee accepted the suggestion of two pies.

The object of this lively competition was a very well-known Texas Mensan named Don Henderson, farmer, cowboy, wine connoisseur and blood-drive promoter. His name first came to my attention by way of an advertisement in the personal columns of *The Bulletin*, (American Mensa's official magazine), to join him at his sun- and fun-filled ranch in Texas. Dark haired, tanned and dressed in my idea of typical Texan garb, he stood on the platform awaiting the gooey pies. Suddenly, quick as a flash, he whipped off his shirt and pants and stood there in his swim suit and boots. Much whooping and hollering greeted this and, as the pies hit, he took it on the chin with a grin and then all over the rest of him as well. He was, however, to have the last laugh the next day.

A very worthwhile event which took place on the last night of the weekend was the MERF auction. MERF is the Mensa Education and Research Foundation; its President is Henry Schofield Noble. It provides funds for scholarships and research and Henry and his committee work extremely hard for the cause, one of Mensa's many benevolent faces. This was the first time the auction had been held at an AG and the many and varied items donated reaped good rewards.

Amongst the items on offer were a jar of ashes from Mount St Helens and a computer printer. An opal and diamond ring drew admiring glances and a crocheted duck who obligingly laid jelly-bean eggs earned smiles. Autographed books, teak elephants from India, hand-knitted afghans, computer software, antique glass and Canada-goose pillows followed each other in swift succession. A massage, a gold bracelet, a camera and Mensa baseball jackets found takers. One particular thing that remained in my mind was the auctioning of a five-dollar bill. Joe Zanca, a fast and smooth talker, was the auctioneer. Bids were made for the note and this continued until there were only two bidders left. They competed against each other until only one remained. However, as both of them had to pay the amount of their final offer, the determination actually to win the five dollars, now out of all proportion, generated much hilarity and eager encouragement. MERF benefited greatly and we all thoroughly enjoyed the exercise. During the auction I noticed one lady energetically running up and down collecting the cash for bids and delivering items purchased. As she passed the aisle where we were sitting I glanced down and saw she was wearing trainers with her beautiful beaded cocktail dress – full marks for practicality.

As International Chairman David was anxious to make a contribution to the event. He had approached the Irish national airline, Aer Lingus, for their help. They generously donated two return tickets, New York to Ireland. The Doyle Group of Hotels, Jury's Hotel and the Shelbourne Hotel equally generously promised accommodation wherever or whenever it was required. Assured of this valuable package David wrote to inform the committee of its contents. They were delighted with the gift and decided that a raffle was the best way of attaining its worth rather than the auction.

With a strategically placed table and joined by willing helpers we had a lot of fun selling the tickets. One particularly bubbly and gregarious girl, studying for her accountancy degree, hauled people in with all the consummate skill of a fisherman; her enthusiasm and persuasiveness allowed very few to escape. Many of the eager punters asked questions about Ireland and the trip. Undoubtedly the strangest enquiry came from someone who asked me whether she would be able to see the bombing if she won the prize. We fervently prayed that she was joking. It was very flattering but not surprising the number of people, many of Irish descent, who were hankering to visit the Emerald Isle.

Towards the end of the auction I was asked to pick the winning ticket for the raffle. The name of the winner? Don Henderson. As I left the platform to return to my seat I realised that I had faced a room full of people without a qualm, something I could never have done before joining Mensa. I had indeed been one of the 'wallpaper Mensans'.

Armadillo racing was an intriguing item on the programme and we followed the crowd to the hall where the races were to be held. A long track had been placed on the floor; it was surrounded and divided in half by a wire mesh and the funny-looking, armour-plated armadillos were meandering around the open cage prior to the 'race'. Encouragement was shouted as they toddled along, helped by the competitors who blew air on to their backs in order to speed them along their meshed tracks. Armadillos are used to getting out of the way of speeding cars; they can move quite quickly if they have to. They were petted and fussed over and appeared to enjoy themselves as much as their audience did. I did not have much success when it was my turn to be a 'jockey', but it was fun seeing the Chairman of Swedish Mensa, Goran Pettersson, enjoying himself immensely, flat on the ground blowing so hard on the rear quarters of his armadillo that its feet hardly touched the ground on the way to the winning post.

A psychiatrist attending the gathering wished to share her frustration about 'Mensa's notorious hedonistic orientation and minimal wish to make any sort of intelligence-related contribution'. Anyone reading the last couple of paragraphs might find this a fair comment. She invited members to join her for a discussion entitled 'High IQ: What it can do for you'. Her accusation appeared to be harsh as so many Mensa people are high achievers, and use their abilities, opportunities and talents intelligently.

One of the questions most frequently asked at any gathering of Mensans is not 'What is your IQ?' but 'What do you do?' As a full-time housewife and mother, I had decided to pre-empt the enquiry by wearing a beautifully scribed badge (made for me by Aidan Lawler, the husband of a member of Irish Mensa, whose hobby is calligraphy) stating my name and occupation – 'Laundress to the Chairman'. This brought me three job offers and an enquiry as to whether I did windows! During a break from the ticket selling I went to have a coffee in the hospitality suite. A very relaxed lady, Phyllis Mechem from Kansas, joined me and, as we chatted, I thought how nice to meet someone so relaxed, easygoing and obviously a home maker like myself – no pressures here. Reluctantly ending the conversation to return to my ticket selling, I could not resist asking her if she worked outside her home. She did, she was an engineer with Boeing.

During our conversation I had vaguely noticed someone standing a few feet away looking in our direction and, as I said goodbye to Phyllis, a blue-jeaned girl wearing one of those tee-shirts which take half an hour to read, caught up with me and asked me why I considered it necessary to defend the fact that I was a woman by wearing such a badge. Was I not ashamed? She went on to inform me that she would not wash shirts for any man, would not demean herself by cooking, nor would she become a slave to anyone. Frankly, looking at her and listening to her views, I didn't think she was in any imminent danger of being asked to do so. (Hell hath no fury like a Schulman scorned.) I was somewhat surprised by the attack and had to think on my feet. 'I wear it as a badge of honour,' I lied (I hate ironing). 'I also clean shoes!' She had no answer to this and with a look of pity for this poor misguided soul, she left.

It would be wrong to give the impression that this weekend consisted solely of one noisy social event after another. Many informative lectures and discussions were held on subjects ranging from technology to psychology, finance to fitness and current affairs to air currents at the swimming pool.

Much good work was being carried out in the form of workshops and a testing session for gifted children. The participants in this area included educators, psychologists, parents and, of course, the children themselves. Two tireless workers for and with the gifted are Dr Dot Funk-Werblo and John B. Ceccherelli. Dot is a gentle and soft-voiced lady who was Chairman of the Gifted Children at this AG, and was renowned for her work in this area and a film she had compiled on the subject. David, having had many enquiries over the years from parents, educators and journalists, asked her for a copy of the film, which he felt would be of help and great interest to a number of Irish people. On his return, he approached the national television network in order to try to get it shown in Ireland. The television pundits, however, did not share his enthusiasm, but it is hoped they may change their minds in the future.

John Ceccherelli, National Co-ordinator for Gifted Children, was equally charming and easy company. A round-faced man with a permanent but genuine smile, he headed a panel of experts who discussed topics such as 'Fears, aspirations and concerns of the gifted'. Pre-teens and teenagers were encouraged to take part and air their views, and John's gentle and friendly manner made it easier for shy and hesitant children to speak up. He was certainly a most popular figure with children and adults alike.

Niki Wenger was the keynote speaker. NASA's teacher in space, she had spent two years away from home, family, friends and students while performing her NASA duties. She attended a reception for local group co-ordinators and all interested Mensans and then gave a talk on 'Lessons from space'. At the end of these sessions she was surrounded by those wanting to ask questions and give their views. There were workshops for people interested in forming groups, and an in-depth report on services, facilities and schools available to the parents of the gifted.

A diverse programme for Young Mensans was available. 'Creating the future' was a challenge to the younger generation to begin to create a better future for all of us. This was held in two parts, with a twenty-four hour break for ideas and solutions to be presented. It would have been most interesting to attend; however, it was open to Young Mensans only and we were precluded by a few years. Computer affairs, auto mechanics – the tricks of the trade, arts and future science, a discussion on sexually-transmitted diseases entitled 'Garfield is a sexy animal' were just a few of the subjects available exclusively to the young Ms. They, of course, were free to attend all events on the programme.

A blood drive, dedicated to the memory of Texas Mensans who had passed away during the year, was eagerly supported. Many new donors were enlisted and the empty-arm established contributors flocked to donate their gift of life. It is but a short step from blood doning to blood curdling. A horror story reading at midnight was the eerie promise of the vampire Special Interest Group. As I tend to watch creepy films through parted fingers, we refrained from attending.

Advice and help was available to individuals running local groups: guidance in the production and distribution of newsletters, membership development, local group finances, special-interest-group administration and all aspects of Mensa. They also had the opportunity to meet the international officers and the American Mensa committee proctor, Dr Abby Salny. Abby is the National and International Supervisory Psychologist. She is, amongst other things, responsible for maintaining testing standards throughout the world and is a devout and devoted Mensan. Despite her busy schedule, she finds time to produce quiz and puzzle books and donates a generous portion of her royalties to MERF. I first met Abby and her charming husband Jerry in London prior to the ruby anniversary but, due to my predilection for smoking and her dislike of it, we did not spend a lot of time together – my loss, I'm sure.

Did you hear the one about the ...? Popular at the gatherings is the 'joke-off'. An official opportunity to elicit laughter was the description given of this get-together. There were Mensans sitting on every available piece of furniture and on the floor when the story and joke telling began. It was run as an informal competition and judged subjectively. So numerous were the eager and budding comedians that it was difficult to get a hearing. Good-natured hissing and booing greeted the corny gags, appreciative laughter the newer and better ones.

Two items appearing on the schedule were, at the time, of little interest to me. One was a bridge tournament, the other a demonstration and talk about cartooning. Very shortly after this AG I took up bridge, becoming hooked immediately, and a couple of years later, I began compiling cartoon-illustrated puzzle books. Today I would not have missed either event. The room allocated to the bridge tournament was Tenison B. Was it a spelling mistake or a deliberate error that made it appear in the brochure as Tension B?

For the fleet of foot, oriental and Middle-Eastern dancing was available. Background history and demonstrations were on tap (sic). Neither David nor I saw any future for us as belly dancers, so we did have a look at the alternative, country and western dancing, but as there are not too many hoe-downs in the Dublin area we finally opted for an hour at the pool instead.

Various musical presentations threaded their way through the weekend. A live band provided entertainment for the formal dance and a pianist provided soothing music for those of a gentler nature. Members were encouraged to play the piano and bring their instruments for impromptu jam sessions. The Gilbert and Sullivan SIG removed their pinafores and introduced the Dallas Gilbert and Sullivan Society with their performance of *Trial by Jury*.

The sheer size of the gathering really manifested itself at lunch in an enormous room on the second day. Having had breakfast at eight o'clock with David and my new-found friend, Oliver North, I felt a bit strange sitting down to lunch at 11.30. I had barely wiped away the crumbs of my new addiction, feather-light cheese croissants, when I found myself faced with a strange phenomenon, the hero sandwich, affectionately known as the 'sub' because of its submarine shape. Subs consist of a huge piece of crispy bread, at least a foot long (305 mm for the 'metric-literate'); cocktail sticks act as scaffolding to hold the assorted toppings in place. Was it possible to eat this without getting lockjaw?

As always when Mensans eat together, there is more emphasis on conversation than food and not knowing how to tackle the monster sandwich I waited patiently for guidance. Our fellow diners picked at the various toppings, drank their coffee and, more importantly, talked. I could only follow suit. When lunch was over and we were discussing the agenda for the afternoon I happened to glance up and the waiters had their trays piled skyscraper high with uneaten torpedo-shaped rolls. I was convinced that twice as many were being returned to the kitchen as had left it.

'Right brain/left brain', 'What is artificial intelligence?', 'A visit to Southfork Ranch', 'Magic', 'Bawdy Broads' reception', 'Tour of Olla Podira', an area close to the hotel, were just a few of the temptations on offer, all within one-and-a-half hours. Having defected from my raffle ticket selling earlier in the morning to attend a 'Sherlock Holmes centenary get-together', I suffered pangs of conscience. I slunk past the 'International update on nuclear energy' meeting room and returned to business at my table.

By this time, the rush for tickets had slowed to a trickle; some enthusiasts returned to buy extra tickets and a girl named Jean from New York paid us a third visit. She told us that she and a friend had visited Ireland the previous year, they had enjoyed every minute of their stay and were determined to return.

They had toured the usual places of interest and many of the beauty spots. Anxious to see the heart of the country after a week of regimented sightseeing, they shunned the available tours and hired a car. Footloose and fancy free they went wherever the mood took them. Driving through Killarney one evening they saw a roadside advertisement for bed and breakfast. Following the signs they found themselves at a lovely old stone farmhouse. It was, she remembered, exactly what she had imagined a typical Irish farm would be: hens scratching in the yard, cows grazing in the field, pigs squealing somewhere in the distance and children playing in the little garden in front of the attractive farmhouse. As they reached the door a woman came out to greet them and they asked her if she had rooms for a couple of nights. She had, and invited them to come in and make themselves at home. 'I will never forget the smell of the baking bread in that big cosy kitchen. You could hear my stomach rumbling all the way back to New York,' said Jean.

There were no other guests staying at the farm so they had their choice of rooms. They asked the farmer's wife to recommend somewhere to eat that night and she suggested a couple of places; however, she added, if they cared to, they would be welcome to join the family and take pot luck with them instead. They cared to – very much. It was a wonderful evening. They told the family of their life in New York and the family filled them in with details of their life at the farm, their guests and their ghost. 'Not a real ghost?' Jean's friend had asked. 'Yes, a real ghost,' answered one of the children. 'We have never seen it, but there is one here.'

It had grown late and the farmer ordered the children to bed; the two girls went outside to stretch their legs. 'The night air was so sweet,' Jean continued, 'we were almost intoxicated by it.' They had had a long day and were tired when they climbed the stairs to their rooms. Half asleep and half awake Jean thought she had heard someone scratching at her door. 'Who is it?' she asked, but receiving no answer she drifted off to sleep. A tapping noise awoke her with a start. She heard a piercing scream followed by a clanking sound. With her heart in her mouth she got out of bed and went to the door; very slowly she eased it open and looked down the long dark corridor. She jumped as her friend, also startled by the noise, appeared at her side. Jean, who described herself as a practising coward, asked her friend to stay with her for a few minutes till her heart returned to its rightful position. As they conjectured what could have shocked them awake, a thumping sound followed by a loud crash sent them running to the door. Wrenching it open they caught a glimpse of a white figure just as it turned the corner at the end of the dim corridor. They could not believe their eyes and stood rooted to the spot. The silence was broken by renewed tapping. Jean does not know where their courage came from but the two of them tiptoed along the dark passage following the sound. 'Tap, tap, tap,' they heard and, peering cautiously around the corner, saw a white-sheeted figure standing at a door. 'Mammy,' whispered the small muffled voice, 'can I finish haunting now, I'm tired and I want to go to bed?' Jean collected her ticket and with a wide grin disappeared into the ever-moving crowd in the big lobby.

The most formal affair of the weekend was the grand dinner which took place on the last full day of the gathering. Incorporated in the social event were the richly deserved accolades and acknowledgements given to the hard-working committee members and volunteers of American Mensa. If you have ever been trapped in your seat at a function and required to contribute your often bored applause, you may be pleased to adopt the 'Cleveland clap', a method used that evening. It sounds like some dreaded disease, but was, in fact, an abridged form of acclaim – one clap per person. Strict adherence to the rule speeded the proceedings along at a galloping rate. Dress at such dinners is, to say the least, mixed. There was everything from jeans to ballgowns (and that was only the men); people simply wore what they wanted to, some of them turning up in lively individual fashions.

The weekend was finally drawing to a close. As I left the courtesy suite for the last time I hoped Oliver would survive without my support. Some people who had driven long distances to Dallas were preparing for their journey home with goodbyes and promises to keep in touch. We were not due to leave for Montreal, the next leg of our journey, until later in the afternoon so we made our way to the American Mensa Committee business meeting. Amy Shaughnessy, minus her shampoo bottle, was joined by Art Mattson, Treasurer of American Mensa, whom we had met previously in Oxford.

Questions directed at Amy came thick and fast. Some members needed facts clarified, others put forward suggestions for consideration and the odd one or two, with a more contentious manner, were dealt with quietly. Amy was admirably cool; she did not allow anything to ruffle her. She provided an object lesson in assertiveness without aggression.

'Deep in the Heart of Taxes', 'The Lady and the Cramp', 'A Vampire's Work is Never Done', 'Trivial Pursuit', a five-and-seven-legged race (Mensans do not do things by halves), 'Magic of the tarot', a fashion show, the movie theatre – the list was endless. We were on the go from early in the morning until late at night but it was impossible to attend everything that appealed to us. For David, beginning his term of office as International Chairman, the AG was a most enlightening experience and a perfect opportunity to meet members and the committee of American Mensa; for me it provided the often-talked-about names with faces. It gave both of us the chance to become part of the sprawling Mensa family.

Farewells completed we started our short trip to the airport. It occurred to me that not once during our stay had we set eyes on Judge Fite, the man who, nine long months before, had introduced us to the gathering, la Republica de Tejas. With so many people, and so many things happening at the same time, I suppose it was only too easy for our paths not to cross. Had they done so, I would have liked to have said to him, 'Judge, after judgemental deliberation we have judged that your judicial judgment was judicious.' In other words, we had a ball.

CHAPTER 6

The sun never sets on Mensa

'Bring bread, cheese, coffee, tea, toilet rolls and any other luxuries you need,' was the advice of a university dean in Moscow to Ed Vincent, International Mensa's Executive Director. Preparing to go to Russia in 1992 for publicity and testing sessions Ed shunned the usual expensive Intourist hotels and was delighted instead to use the dean's help to secure a tiny apartment for his visit. 'Not only will this save money,' he said, 'but it will mean that I can live amongst the people themselves.'

International Mensa embraces all parts of the globe. It is the umbrella organisation under which all National Mensas shelter. Among its responsibilities are the strict maintenance of testing standards and the furtherance of the aims of Mensa worldwide. The members, numbering over 100,000, can be found in more than one hundred countries. Most of them are in the larger, fully-recognised Mensas and the remainder either in countries where there are provisional Mensas, awaiting full recognition, or loosely distributed around the globe.

The International Board of Directors (IBD) comprises an elected body of four people, the Chairman, Director of Administration, Director of Development and the Treasurer, together with the chief executive officers of the recognised National Mensas. As the membership grows within a country there is an entitlement to extra votes and additional National Representatives (NatReps) are required. This additional allotment of NatReps currently only affects the American and British Mensas. Those Mensas which are not large enough to qualify for a seat on the board are entitled to representation on the international general council (IGC).

If you are now thoroughly confused don't worry, it will get worse!

The office of International Mensa is situated in London and is administered by Ed Vincent, the Executive Director, and his staff. Ed is a gregarious, capable, humorous and much-travelled administrator. In the last two years alone he has covered a prodigious amount of territory visiting: India, Romania, Poland, Russia, Czechoslovakia, Yugoslavia, Bulgaria, Turkey, 'Lisbon and Limerick' (his quote, not mine!).

Ed is an American, who moved to London to head a branch of an American college (which he founded). Born and educated in New York, he gained an MA in literature and then, seeking fresh fields of endeavour, began his career as a teacher. He became a lecturer and then an administrator. Changing course, he entered the world of marketing as a manager for a large producer of wines and spirits, wrote comedy programmes for American television (given his excellent sense of humour this did not come as too much of a surprise to me), became a published poet and still enjoys writing in the odd minutes that Mensa does not need him. His main task is the development of Mensa, which he has represented in twenty-five countries so far and has made friends and promoted good will in – twenty-seven of them. He has started groups in Hong Kong, Poland, Singapore, Romania, Indonesia and Bulgaria and, he claims, in order to be totally international, Mensa needs to penetrate further into Asia, Africa and South America.

Carol Rickard, personal assistant to the executive director, has displayed her talents on Mensa's behalf. She has been responsible for testing and public relations in Pakistan, Colombia and Indonesia and she will in the near future travel to Karachi.

The hardships some of the enthusiasts from Eastern Europe endure are an indication of their eagerness to become part of this Western-based society. While testing was taking place in Belgrade so many people turned up that it was impossible to process them all in one day. Undaunted, although many of them had travelled long distances and had very little money, several of the remaining untested candidates slept out in parks, presenting themselves for the test the following day with no word of complaint.

To highlight national differences I cannot resist mentioning something that happened in Dublin prior to a test session. Somebody telephoned one Saturday morning to say they would not be able to attend the test session arranged for them that day at the University as, it appeared, there was a strong possibility that it would rain. It was discovered subsequently that this person lived about two hundred metres from the gates of the campus!

In Warsaw over a thousand people were clamouring to be tested. Returning to Warsaw some time later for Mensa Poland's inaugural meeting, Ed Vincent and David, who accompanied him in his capacity as International Chairman, were welcomed with enormous courtesy and kindness by a couple, Jola and Andrzej Urbanik, who had organised the necessary publicity and made all the arrangements for the testing sessions. Mensa Poland has an enthusiastic following and one of its members, Janus Majewski, heads the Polish Film Institute.

In Bucharest a university lecturer named Daniel Serbanica and his wife Alina read of Mensa and wrote for details. Daniel arranged to take the test by post, under supervision; he scored well and accepted the offer of membership. Each month he received a copy of the Mensa *International Journal* and his copy of *Isolated M*. After some months he learnt that his mail had been intercepted and one day two men from the Securitate knocked at his door. They had come to question him about this 'intelligence organisation' to which he belonged. He explained that Mensa was non-political, non-ideological and they finally seemed satisfied. Today he and his wife run Romanian Mensa and are an extremely popular and well-liked couple. They have written, produced, and distributed a 30-page magazine with a circulation of 100,000, the profits of which are distributed to various charities in Romania. The constitution of Mensa Romania has now been approved and the membership is growing steadily.

There are now many members in Eastern Europe and, no doubt, with the new political freedom their numbers will increase rapidly in the near future. At the IBD meeting in Budapest, Hungary, in the autumn of 1991, board members were delighted by the large attendance of Eastern European delegates. The meeting was one of the largest that the board had ever held. Originally it was to have been held in Zagreb, but the rapid build-up of internal strife in Yugoslavia dictated a fairly late change of venue. Troubled Yugoslavia had no representative at the meeting, at least not for the first hour. Then the door of the meeting room opened and a figure appeared apologising for his late arrival – Josip Saban, the chairman from Yugoslavia. He informed the board that he had had no intention of missing the meeting, so had climbed out of his cellar, where for the previous couple of days he had been sheltering from the gunfire and the bombs, got into his car and just drove and drove until he reached the border, having passed through five checkpoints, each manned by either semi-official or self-appointed militia. His courage and determination impressed all who were there and, perhaps even more, his reply to the question whether he intended returning home. 'Of course. While we are alive life must continue and my country will need all its people.' In the short time that has elapsed since that meeting, Mensa Yugoslavia has been fragmented into: Mensa Croatia, Mensa Slovenia, Mensa Serbia, Montenegro, Bosnia etc?

My introduction to International Mensa was in Dublin. In conjunction with the Irish annual gathering, Ireland hosted the meeting of the IBD and IGC. The International Board members strive to keep expenses to a minimum, and eschew luxurious junkets. Naturally, no spouses (should it not be spice?) are catered for by Mensa and if they should accompany their wives or husbands it is entirely at their own expense.

The recently refurbished de luxe Shelbourne Hotel had been having prolonged strike trouble at the same time as undergoing a costly and extensive face-lift, Mensa was able to take advantage of this quiet and troubled time to reserve rooms at an absolute 'steal'. The hotel provided a hospitality suite, and Tomorrow's World, a firm which sells all types of computers, kindly installed a bank of ZX Sinclair computers and software for the members' amusement. Such was the enthusiasm generated by the computer games that we learnt to recognise people by the backs of their heads. The Lord Mayor gave a reception at the Mansion House and the Irish Tourist Board hosted a reception at the beautiful, newly-opened National Concert Hall. With true Mensa organisation the spring sun shone gloriously for the entire weekend and the trees and bushes in St Stephen's Green, the park immediately opposite the hotel, vied with each other to see which could produce the most coats of green.

For one English couple it was a bonus that at least the days were warm as they were camping in a small tent. Even though they wore every stitch of their clothing, they found the nights bitterly cold. If they had contacted the Irish SIGHT officer they would have fared much better – but more of SIGHT later.

Prior to the busy weekend I had been expecting the board members representing the various countries to be superhuman. Furthermore, languages are not my strong suit, so it was with trepidation that I greeted them on the evening of their arrival at a buffet party we held at home to welcome them to Ireland. Wrong again – they were normal, friendly people, all speaking excellent English (particularly the British contingent). The International Treasurer, Len Rickard, was accompanied by his delightful wife, Sue. She had been a cross-country skier and we were sad to learn that she was suffering from multiple sclerosis. We admired her determination to enjoy her short stay in Ireland and her attitude to life in general. During the weekend there was an earthquake in the San Francisco area where they lived and, quite naturally, Sue was apprehensive when she telephoned relations to find out if their home had suffered damage; fortunately, all was well.

The International Chairman at that time was Hyman Brock, four times city councillor and Pro-Mayor of Montreal. He and his wife Barbara were making their first trip to Ireland and our paths, I am happy to say, have crossed many times since then.

When David took over the chairmanship of Mensa International from Hyman the transition seemed to involve many, many phone calls, letters and discussions. The calls usually came from Hyman in the evening, often at dinner time, and sometimes much later. As we enjoyed rubber bridge the calls often interrupted games and, after some time, when the phone rang during a game our partners would chorus, 'It's Hyman.' We used to chat amongst ourselves while David was taking the calls, which could last a long time. On one such evening the phone rang and was greeted by the usual chorus; quite correctly they had guessed it was Hyman. There were many problems to be discussed; the call went on and on until, finally, our partners decided it was getting too late to continue the game, packed up and went home. That was the last of the interrupted bridge games. The Riot Act was read to David and he reluctantly told Hyman what had happened. Hyman took it in very good part, and from then on always enquired whether it was convenient or whether he should call back at another time.

New members of the Board chatted to one another, told stories, even exchanged recipes and all our guests, including those who were jet-lagged, managed to relax and enjoy the evening. I had the extra pleasure of identifying the people about whom David had so often spoken.

The following day, while the Board of Directors met to discuss its lengthy agenda, Irish Mensa held its Annual General Meeting and British Mensa conducted one of its committee meetings, which had been arranged to coincide with this exciting event. A most unusual selection of meetings and a 'first' in Mensa's history.

The visitors enjoyed the social programme provided by the hardworking Irish Mensa Committee. As well as the official receptions and dinner, there was a Chinese banquet, a jazz concert, ten-pin bowling, a tour of Dublin, shopping, and a particularly enjoyable treasure hunt held at the Dublin Zoo.

Almost fifty per cent of the population of the Republic of Ireland (3,523,401 people for those who like figures) is under twenty-four years of age, and I am sure that Irish Mensa (both North and South) would have a higher percentage of young members than many of the other national groups.

It was at this gathering that an Irish Mensan announced that her marriage to a British Mensan had taken place that morning. What better place to spend a honeymoon?

At the reception hosted by Bord Failte (the Irish Tourist Board) in the magnificent circular gallery of the Concert Hall, members wandered around talking to friends and visitors, the committee members relaxed and the press collected their stories. One ingenuous young girl, the guest of a member, approached the Chairman of British Mensa, Sir Clive Sinclair. 'Is that you, yourself?' she enquired. Clive's sense of humour immediately manifested itself: 'No, no, it's not me,' he replied, 'it's just a cardboard cut-out.'

The gala dinner that followed this reception was held in the foyer of the Concert Hall. The lofty ceiling with its magnificent Waterford glass chandelier and the tastefully appointed tables created a formal but happy atmosphere. Some of the delegates when making their speeches used their native language; simultaneous translation was provided by the director of development, Katia Chestapolov, an international civil servant working for the World Meteorological Organisation at the UN in Geneva. Her linguistic ability was breathtaking; green with envy, we listened to her switching from one language to another with total ease. This was the only time I have heard any language other than English being spoken at an International Gathering.

Generally board members see very little of the cities they visit; they tend to find themselves in conference hotels situated out of town and thus have little or no opportunity for sightseeing. This struck me forcibly when attending the International meeting in London, chosen on that occasion to coincide with the Ruby Anniversary celebrations.

Members of the board and representatives arrived from all parts of the globe in time for the first meeting to be held in London on the Thursday afternoon. They went straight to the meeting and left for Oxford on the Monday morning without having had an opportunity to see anything of London. Similar situations have arisen in countries all over the Mensa world and so, on becoming International Chairman, David proposed that half a day should be set aside for a tour of the city hosting the meeting. Needless to say this was a popular proposal for those whose time was strictly limited, and now it has become the tradition that Sunday morning is set aside for an organised coach tour, complete with guide. Being a guide on a bus full of Mensans is not an enviable task. Often some of the passengers know more about the history of the city and of the country than the guide does, and they are not slow to correct any factual errors. This is not done in a superior way, but many Mensans are very keen on receiving correct information. (I have no doubt that Mensans reading this are already reaching for their word processors to fire a few shots across my bows.)

When the London meeting's business finished for the day, we went to eat at a local restaurant. We were a somewhat noisy bunch, occupying two large tables. Spanish music in the background prompted Catherine Ford, Canadian President at that time (and always game for a laugh), to take the rose from the vase on the table and her shyly reluctant fiancé from his chair, to give her rendition of a *paso doble*. As a dancer, she made a good journalist! As we were leaving the restaurant an American couple who had been sitting at the next table stopped me. They said they had thoroughly enjoyed all the chatter and laughter and asked which group we were with? When I said, 'Mensa', I was amused to see two jaws drop open simultaneously.

Philadelphia was the venue of the next IBD and IGC meeting that I attended. Combining it with a holiday we intended to spend three or four days in Washington. We contacted Amy Shaughnessy and her husband David Hume and several other Mensans we knew in the area, all of whom were most welcoming. Amy and David took us out to dinner and then to a meeting of Washington Mensa.

As they arrived to collect us we saw for the first time a car with 'MENSA' as a registration plate. We then experienced our first tasty Vietnamese meal, very different from anything we had ever eaten. A large bowl of boiling hot broth was brought to each diner, this was accompanied by bowls of finely diced vegetables and plates of shaved, paper thin meats. The meats and vegetables were placed into the bowls of steaming liquid and in seconds they were cooked. Enormous numbers of people were coming and going in the busy restaurant; obviously Vietnamese food was highly popular.

We were again made very welcome by members who were holding their local election meeting and, when we finally arrived in Philadelphia, we recognised a lot of the members we had met in Washington that evening.

The meetings started early the next morning and I did not hurry to have breakfast. David returned to the room to collect his document case and told me that there was a restaurant serving breakfast two doors away from the hotel and suggested I should try it. It was the epitome of an American film 'diner'. Seating myself in a booth with its immovable table, the lone waitress yelled, 'With you in a minute Hon!' Hon waited. 'Hi Hon!' she declared, and without asking, she cheerfully slopped coffee into the cup, the saucer and on to the table. It was the most enjoyable breakfast time I have had for years. She served the whole of the busy diner, chatting with the construction workers who had broken into their morning to have breakfast. She advised them what to order – whether they wanted it or not. In loud tones she enquired about families and their problems from the obvious regulars (forcing me to strain in order to hear all their responses) kept a wary eye on my cup which by then was almost invisible in an avalanche of brown-stained napkins. Here white orthopaedic shoes had become artistically decorated with brown splashes as she mothered the starving masses with her precariously tilted jug of steaming liquid. As I left the cosy atmosphere her final yell of, 'Have a good day, Hon,' was supplemented by 'Missing you already'. No wonder David recommended it – and how well he knows me and my sense of elegance.

Our three days in Washington stretched to ten days, and although the autumn leaves had turned their glorious colours, the temperature was in the high eighties. We had listened to advice and geared ourselves with warm sweaters and coats; we melted as we made our way through the many galleries and museums – enjoying every overheated minute of it. Should you ever want to take a trip and experience unseasonal weather, join us, we manage to do it every time.

The meeting in Philadelphia was held in conjunction with the regional gathering (RG). This was well attended and members were pleased and interested to meet so many foreign visitors. The hospitality suites were open at all hours, stocked with food nibbles and drinks and, as always, good company – the by now familiar, friendly faces.

Helen Kupper, the Director of Administration, arrived with my annual fix of vanilla-bean coffee. This is unavailable in Ireland; we hoard it in our freezer and dole it out in very meagre amounts to lovers of real coffee. Coffee apart, Helen was a kind and good friend to us and a tireless worker for Mensa.

Velma Jeremiah, then International Treasurer, arrived with a suitcase as big as she was, and certainly heavier, containing her reports.

Also toting heavy cases – Udo Schultz, Mensa Germany's representative and International Director of Development. Udo's cases, however, contained his ever-present photographic equipment. This smiling-faced mustachioed man is a popular figure among the delegates and it must be stated that, even in Mensa, it is rare to find a German telling jokes in English with a Welsh accent. This Uso does to perfection. Born in Kiel, the capital of Schleswig-Holstein, he became acquainted with the English language at a very early stage when his aunt married a British soldier who was stationed in Kiel. Having finished school Udo started a three year training period as a Civil Servant. He worked in the Board of Fisheries and in the Computer Centre of Schleswig-Holstein, holding the position of Directors Assistant. At present Udo is in the Marketing Department and occasionally teaches Computer English.

Having successfully solved a mini-test in *Reader's Digest* he subsequently mastered the Mensa admission test and became a member of Mensa in Deutschland. Attending his first AG in Cologne he met a girl, Sigi, who later became his wife. They now have two daughters, Megan Mareike and Arwen Amelie. Their names Udo says, 'reflecting our love for that beautiful part of the globe, Wales.'

Serving as Local Secretary and then Chairman of German Mensa Udo acts as proctor – testing perspective candidates in his local area. Media interest in Mensa has resulted in many interviews: television, radio and newspapers and has increased awareness and membership substantially.

For the benefit of local members Udo and Sigi edit a magazine which augments the national magazine, *Bagatelle*. In the summer of 1991 he arranged one of the first MensaMATE programmes (similar to the 'twinning' system so popular today) between Mensa Schleswig-Holstein and Mensa/Fyn-Denmark. The family activities largely revolve around Mensa as Sigi is responsible for organising the testing activities of approximately forty proctors, giving them advice when needed. Sigi is also Treasurer for the Mensa Selection Agency.

When time permits Udo's hobbies and interests include; family, house and garden, photography and video, travel – mainly to Wales – meeting friends and singing in the local church choir.

There is always something to be learned in Mensa. Lesson for today is that the students university canteen is called 'Mensa' in several areas of Europe. This has resulted in the past in some very odd requests from people; an applicant experienced in running professional kitchens applied for a job, a phone call requesting that Udo should search for an umbrella which had been left in the Mensa after a celebration the previous evening and, towards the end of the year, they could have done a roaring trade with people booking for New Year's Eve parties in the Mensa.

The meeting came to an end at 6.30 and arrangements were made for anyone who was interested to go out to eat to meet in the lobby at 7.30. As always, there was a large contingent. The Mayor of Philadelphia declared a Mensa week and we were given a talk by a most charming and able representative from his office.

Visitors are permitted to attend IBD and IGC meetings, so the following day, as I was eager to hear David chairing the meeting, I spent some considerable time there and found it fascinating. Each national Mensa had a say in the proceedings and each had a mixture of successes and failures to report and discuss. The time flew by as subject after subject was debated and dealt with.

Dealing with the problems of individual countries is always a large part of the board's duties. Communications, encouraging membership, economic problems (particularly in the Eastern European countries), protection of members' rights, policy decisions, future courses of action, maintenance of the constitution – these were but a few of the items on a packed agenda. David presided, sometimes interjecting with his own brand of humour. Hands up whoever said 'biased'.

The high standard of testing must be maintained throughout the world and there are very few International Board Meetings which the Supervisory Psychologist, Abby Salny, who keeps a watchful eye on the correctness of testing procedures, does not attend. Recently Abby negotiated for Mensa the outright purchase of two of the Cattell tests upon which, up until now, Mensa had been charged a royalty for each time a test was used. This will no doubt save Mensa a great deal of money in the years to come.

It was interesting to discover that at some meetings Mensa Switzerland have four languages at their disposal: Italian, French, German and

Romansh. For the sake of their visitors they often conduct their meetings in English.

It was a pleasure to meet more new people during the weekend. Beth Sample, a Californian Mensan, has added sunshine to my life on rainy days and a new word to my vocabulary – 'bumbershoot', an unusual name for an umbrella. Beth, a specialist in family law, was a happy and bright companion and, in truth, a giggler. She had left her legal problems at home, probably in the closet with her bumbershoot, and enjoyed the RG.

Liz and Dave Remine were names I had heard and they became real people to me at Philadelphia. Whilst Dave Remine, American Mensa's hard-working, feet-firmly-on-the-ground, competent Treasurer was at meetings, Liz was studying hard for her second Master's degree, in computer science. She filled in just a little of her spare time holding down two jobs. We were delighted to learn from their 1991 Christmas card that she had attained the second degree with flying colours. Liz and Dave were very good company and I look forward to our next meeting.

A fancy-dress ball followed the banquet held on the Saturday night. The costumes were innovative and raised many an amused eyebrow in the busy hotel; in the lobby a test tube baby could be seen chatting with a skeleton, and they were joined by Edu Braat from Mensa Netherlands, elegantly clad in a black tie, tee-shirt and jeans. We met Edu on a visit we made to Amsterdam last May, when temperatures soared to 4 degrees above freezing. Edu and a friend came to have a drink with us and he brought with him a copy of a new quarterly magazine he had edited. This colourful journal was not Mensa-inspired: its subject matter was teddy bears.

In the foyer after the banquet I was introduced to a member of New York Mensa who claimed to know every lateral-thinking puzzle ever invented. These puzzles are solved by asking questions to which only minimal answers are given. The logical solution is finally reached by process of elimination. I was very impressed by his fund of knowledge but inadvertently ruined his evening, and possibly his reputation, by producing two puzzles of which he had never heard. We were soon joined by several people and spent a frustrating but happy hour trying to solve the various posers.

A guided tour of Philadelphia and a luncheon brought the official RG to a close. The Liberty Bell is undoubtedly the city's most famous landmark and Benjamin Franklin its most famed citizen. A professional actor in authentic costume, and bearing an uncanny resemblance to Benjamin Franklin, gave a most vivid insight into the life and times of the great statesman, writer and inventor. The lightning conductor and bi-focal lenses are two of his better-known innovations and now it is not uncommon to hear spectacles referred to as Ben Franklins.

The RG ended as is customary on a Sunday and the board continued with its meetings. Steve Slepner and his committee had thoughtfully arranged for the hospitality suite to remain open for a further twenty-four hours. A few of us who had returned to the suite later that night were sitting talking when a breathless young man arrived enquiring whether he was too late for the RG. He had been away on assignment he told us and, of course, realising he was a journalist, I asked him if it had been an interesting one. 'Routine,' he said. 'Do you work for a newspaper?' I asked. 'I'm an industrial private detective. You know, spying on the spies, checking boardrooms and telephone systems for bugs. Industrial espionage is rife today.' A natural mistake on my part. However, it was the best exercise that I had had all weekend – jumping to conclusions!

Even though Mensa is spreading rapidly to all four corners of the world (yes, the world is round but I'm speaking metaphorically) there are many countries which, as yet, do not have an established Mensa. Where there is no national organisation people wishing to join Mensa can apply directly to the International office which can arrange testing. Having joined, they receive the *International Journal* which keeps them in touch with the other members and the Mensa activities throughout the world.

Some time ago Mensa made the headlines when an article appeared in *Playboy*. It contained photographs of a group of female members in the nude and their erudite comments and views of life were also exposed. There is now a rumour circulating that the male Mensa Directors have been offered $100 each *not* to appear in the magazine, nude or otherwise!

Some statistics – not lies. The gender breakdown of Mensa membership is two-thirds men and one-third women, but at management level there are more women than men. There has been much speculation as to why there is this enormous discrepancy in the male/female ratio. One theory is that men are more anxious to prove themselves and another is that women feel they have no need to prove themselves. Another fact (one of mine so it is indisputable) is that almost without exception, anyone who takes an IQ test scores higher than they honestly anticipated; we all underestimate our capabilities.

At the IBD meeting in Budapest the increased representation, primarily from the emergent Eastern European Mensans, was greeted with much pleasure. Over forty people represented twenty-five countries. No one could be blamed for being a little puzzled by the various nationalities of some of the representatives. Mensa New Zealand was represented by its Chairman, Piet Van Der Meyden, a Dutchman; Irish Mensa's President carried a British Mensa proxy; Belgian Mensa's NatRep was French; Australia's representative and Chairman, Bill Fisher, is a New Zealander; Jaqueline Berlet from the Channel Islands is French and last, but most certainly not least, Mensa Canada's President, K. H. Wickremasinghe (Wicks), is originally from Sri Lanka. More scope here for theories as to why Mensans move around so much, but you can fill in your own. I have had a heavy run on theories lately and am not prepared to waste any more time on them at the moment.

Neil Goulder, a NatRep and Britain's answer to Bart Simpson, stands six feet six in his psychedelic socks. The International Treasurer, Godwin Zwanenburg, towers over him and clocks in at about six feet ten. The then Canadian President, Wicks, is a slightly-built five foot three, if he is an inch. David described what he said was one of the funniest sights he has seen: the two tall men, hooking their arms through Wicks's, lifted him off the ground till all three heads were more or less level and, with Wicks's tiny feet treading air, the three of them strolled along the streets of Budapest enjoying a conversation.

At the time of writing the next IBD meeting is scheduled for the Netherlands. This will follow the first-ever gathering of Mensans from all over the world. David had hoped to be able to use the deserted Olympic Village in Barcelona, Spain, immediately following the 1992 Olympics, but it was not to be. The enormous logistic problems made the preparations too difficult.

During David's years on the International Board of Directors he has had the privilege of meeting many marvellous people and visiting several countries. Malaysian Mensa's representatives have been outstandingly courteous, friendly, hard working and dedicated. With over 2,000 members it was one of the fastest growing groups in the world until the Berlin Wall came down and the Eastern European countries greeted Mensa with open arms. Over three-quarters of Malaysia's members are under twenty-one years of age.

At the IBD executive meeting held in Kuala Lumpur, Malaysia, a few years ago the committee and members were efficient and hospitable. The business meetings were fruitful and a heavy agenda was routinely dealt with. The local committee had arranged newspaper and TV coverage and the resultant publicity, together with the faith and encouragement that the board had shown in scheduling a meeting for the first time in the Far East, helped produce many new members and consolidated a friendly arrangement with the *Star* newspaper, which has befriended Mensa and run several competitions provided by Mensa.

At the hotel in Kuala Lumpur, as in most of the hotels in the Far East, the service was impeccable; the lifts arrived silently and immediately at the touch of a button. Every night, exactly at midnight, the mats in the lifts were changed; each mat bore the word 'welcome', and the name of the day of the week which, for the often jet-lagged visitors, served as a useful reminder.

One evening the board members were taken to a restaurant some distance from their hotel. The children of the owners scampered up and down staring and giggling at the funny-looking strangers. David, who is always wary about what he eats, enquired of the hosts about the dishes on the circular turntable. 'Don't worry,' they said, 'it is all right. You can eat everything.' They enjoyed their meal and David, complimenting the hosts on their choice of one particularly tasty item, could not discover an English translation of the name of the dish. One of the other visitors decided to wind him up by suggesting it was a toss-up whether it was snake or steak. Either way, heads or tails, it wriggled down quite well.

Some of the International Board visited Hong Kong, others went to Singapore and to Bangkok in order to visit other Mensas and to attend press conferences in the hope of increasing Mensa membership and awareness.

At this time Mensa Singapore did not exist. There were 200 possible members eager to form a National Mensa there, but government rules stated that anyone wanting to form an association of any kind must meet, decide on the aims and objects, rules, regulations, bye-laws and constitution. They must then disband, having presented the details for approval and inspection to the relevant government department. Mensa complied with the necessary requirements, was eventually accepted and is now flourishing.

Bangkok was the last port of call. David, with Barbara and Hyman Brock, contacted the few scattered international members there. Newspaper interviews were held and one expatriate American woman became an enthusiastic supporter but, as yet, Mensa Thailand has still to be born.

Before 'The Wall came tumbling down' there was only one member in East Berlin. He kept in touch through German Mensa who sent him their magazine, *Bagatelle*. It was often intercepted or did not arrive at all. When the IBD held its meeting in Germany all the board members hired a coach and travelled to East Berlin to meet him for tea. He was so overcome with emotion he just broke down and wept (they have that effect on people sometimes). Now of course, he is automatically a member of German Mensa and his years of isolation are over.

One of the most surprising requests made to David on his travels was to meet and talk to the wife of a member who suffered a phobia about Irishmen. David readily agreed to meet her in a neutral place and hoped that by talking to her it would help to reduce her fear.

She said that her father was Irish and had left home when she was very young, so David surmised that some form of abuse, mental or physical, was the cause of her phobia. They arranged to meet in a friendly area away from meetings and other Mensans. The two of them arrived and they chatted amiably and finally David casually mentioned he was from Dublin. Her reaction was frightening, she backed away from him trembling from head to toe. Covering her face with her hands, she wailed and cried, shivered and was utterly terrified. Her husband was unable to do anything to help her; David immediately told her that he only lived in Ireland, but was not Irish, and not to be afraid as he would not harm her in any way. Eventually her shaking stopped and she became calmer and once again they talked and he reassured her that her one bad experience did not in any way represent Irishmen in general. She listened to him and then began to join in the conversation and, after extending an invitation to him to visit their home, she left with her husband.

David hoped that his reassurances had helped her and naturally was concerned lest his presence trigger her fear again. However, when he arrived at their home she was absolutely relaxed and unfearing. She gave him some beautiful sea shells, some of which were hand painted, and David felt fairly confident by the end of his visit that she had accepted what he said as being true; certainly there was no more sign of nervousness in her manner. This was a strange occurrence that pitched David into the unaccustomed role of amateur psychologist.

So the work of the IBD and IGC continues. They look forward to the day that every country in the world is represented in the Mensa family, by which time Ed Vincent will no doubt be holding testing sessions and press conferences on Venus and Mars.

Whilst I have been writing this chapter I have been in constant touch with the international office in London for any interesting updates. Ed Vincent has taken to the hills, the hills of Turkey, in order to escape my calls. Harold Gale, Executive Director of British Mensa, has been in a meeting since last October and Robert Allen, Editorial Director at Mensa Publications, white haired and stooped, was last seen walking around Cambridge supporting himself with a stick and muttering darkly. Congratulations to him on his twenty-ninth birthday!

CHAPTER 7

Bright sparks

'My four-year-old son is running a protection racket in school,' a voice sobbed over the telephone. 'His henchmen, aged five and six, are terrorising the younger children, promising all sorts of retribution if they do not part with their pennies, sweets, and crisps.' This is not a common call to the Irish Mensa office, and let me hasten to add that all I can do with such a call, when David is away, is to lend a sympathetic ear and supply the telephone number of the British Mensa office in Wolverhampton.

A considerable number of parents ask what best to do with their three- or four-year-olds who are already bored with their play schools. Most of these children can read and have a grasp of subjects far beyond their tender years, and in some cases they are so disruptive that the distracted parents are at their wits' end by the time they seek advice.

The only 'A' some parents see on their child's report card is for 'absent', but for others the 'A' is a grade and, delighted by their child's consistently high marks, they contact the office asking for a test, or sometimes they are referred by teachers or psychologists. These children are the lucky ones. Their giftedness has been recognised.

The more distressed parents are often instantly reassured to learn that there are many children with the same behavioural patterns as their own: boredom, attention-seeking and even tantrums being just three of them. Bright children can and do fail to reach their true academic level as a result of peer pressure on them to conform. 'Teacher's pet', 'smartyboots' and 'brain-box' are just a few of the many well-worn jibes classmates can direct at these youngsters, leaving them with the dilemma: should they strive for academic achievement or give in to the very real need to be part of the gang?

Today's bright youngsters are often more fortunate than past scholars. Teachers are conscious of the need to provide educational stimulation for bright children and, with the co-operation of the parents, these frustrated tots-to-teens can settle into a rewarding and happy normalcy.

When we visited Montreal some years ago, Barbara Brock, in her role of hostess and tour guide, made our stay in that beautiful city a most interesting experience. She pointed out various places of civic interest and the school which her young son had attended.

One day, many years ago, she had received a call from her son's teacher demanding that she come to the school and Barbara, fearing that he was ill or had had an accident, rushed there immediately. Her fears proved incorrect, but she was not prepared for the tirade which the teacher delivered. She wasted no time in telling Barbara that her son was totally undisciplined and destined for trouble; he disrupted classes and was everything that was bad in the teacher's eyes. This woman berated Barbara in front of her son, stating that she was unfit to be a mother. At first she was stunned by the attack and then heartbroken. 'I cried for weeks,' she admitted. The next couple of months were made intolerable for the child; he was picked on for everything he did and said in school, he was belittled in front of his classmates and returned home very unhappy each day. It became impossible for him to remain at the school.

He was moved to a nearby public (in the North American sense) school and eventually settled down and completed his education. Despite the happy outcome to the story Barbara, a gentle and tactful person, never forgot the stinging accusation and her agitation was obvious as she repeated it.

Many years later she and her husband Hyman ran across the never-to-be-forgotten teacher at a social function. Barbara confronted her and, regardless of the company present, informed the startled woman that, despite her unfair accusations and predictions, the child that she had condemned so readily was now a highly qualified and respected member of the medical profession who had graduated with the highest possible honours from his university. Barbara added that, although she might hold teaching qualifications, she had no idea of the correct way to approach or communicate with children. With that she turned on her heel and left. Barbara is still not sure who was the more surprised at the vehemence of her retaliation, herself or the teacher, but the unfairness of the original attack, coupled with the teacher's lack of understanding of her child, had rankled for many years. This lack of communication by some teachers is, unfortunately, not particularly rare and, perhaps even more sadly, when a teacher does recognise so-called 'giftedness' he or she is not always able to deal with the child effectively.

Margaret and Kate Kavanagh, two of British Mensa's gifted children, joined the Society following a school psychologist's report. Someone had suggested that their parents contact Mensa for educational advice. The family live in a rural area, do not have a lot of contact with other Mensans and most of the children's free time is taken up with homework. Both sisters play numerous musical instruments: piano, tenor saxophone, flute and clarinet. They wish Mensa had the power to influence teachers to 'teach' instead of constantly telling pupils to look things up.

Margaret and Kate's mother, prior to their younger sister Hannah's birth, was considered 'high risk' from an age point of view; she was assured, on a routine visit to the hospital, that there was some time before the baby was due. Not so, as a newspaper cutting she sent me relates. On the way home she stopped in at a garage for petrol and it became apparent to odd-job man Graham Allen that she was in need of immediate help. He escorted her to the reception area where, after a very short time, the baby arrived. This prompted her mother to call her daughter her 'four-star baby' and the proud garage displayed a new sign in its window stating that 'Pump Hill always delivers on time'. I hope that their eight-year-old sister will also become a member then Mensa too can boast of *Hannah and her sisters*.

The words sizzled with good humour in a letter from A-X-E-L Kenney, an eight-year-old member of Irish Mensa. He had fallen out of his pram with boredom from listening to jokes like 'what has three axles?' and I could, he informed me, call him anything I chose but not Axle. He joined Mensa at the age of six, because his parents were members, and he said he was quite happy to help my research with 'a little pressure from my Dad. Oh the trauma!' He did not have a lot of contact with other Mensa children but, 'at eight, there's not much I can do (street cred and all that) except write to the magazines'. He is, he says, getting ready to run junior Mensa by himself but gets lazy on days with a 'Y' in them. He had spent some time at events run by the National Association of Gifted Children and was looking forward to attending the lectures and workshops, and going on the outings of the newly formed Mensa Foundation for Gifted Children in Northern Ireland. His unusual hobby is collecting silly signs such as the one he spotted in Bangor, Northern Ireland, stating 'Dogs, riding bicycles in the park, prohibited'.

A brief item in the *International Journal* some months ago caught my attention. Sarah McCracken, aged eight, a member of Mensa New Zealand, was to become the youngest pupil in the world-renowned Yehudi Menuhin School of Music. The family were planning to relocate to England in order to be with their daughter. I contacted the headmaster of the school, Nicolas Chisolm, and asked him if he would be willing to forward a letter to Sarah's parents. He was more than helpful and informed me that the family had decided to remain in New Zealand and to let Sarah attend the school. Mr Chisolm gave me their home address.

Sarah's mother, Carol, had always loved music and played records, discs and tapes constantly in their home. When Sarah was two-and-a-half years old the McCrackens took their children to hear a live orchestra. When the first violinist came on to the stage to tune the orchestra Sarah jumped up and asked what the instrument was called. After the concert was over she turned to her mother and said, 'Mummy, I was born to play one of those.' This later became, 'I was born to be a violinist.'

Sarah has had a rough time in New Zealand. 'The country is small and somewhat isolated, and giftedness is not considered to be a virtue,' said Carol and added that, 'Piet Van Der Meyden, Chairman of Mensa New Zealand, has had an uphill battle trying to keep the society and its allied interest in gifted children on its feet.'

One day, at the age of three, Sarah was sitting in a park reading a book. A man who had noticed her total absorption came up and asked her what the book was about. She showed it to him and he was surprised to see that it had no pictures. He then asked her to read part of it to him, which she did. He talked to her at length and discovered that she could write as well as read. It transpired that he held a doctorate in education and he and the McCrackens became good friends; he helped Sarah with her education until his death eighteen months later. It was on his advice that they approached the Gifted Children's Association but they found it somewhat limiting. Someone there told them that they should contact Piet Van Der Meyden, who suggested that Sarah take an IQ test. At four years of age she was qualified to join Mensa.

She started kindergarten, but after one week it was more than obvious that she was not going to fit in, so her parents arranged for her to go to a school one day a week. That did not work out either, so her mother began to teach her at home. When Sarah turned five they tried her at another school one day a week, then two, and by the time she reached the three-day mark she refused to go back. She had been given the name of 'baby smarty-pants'; her classmates were two and three years her senior and she was still bored stiff as she found the work so simple.

A psychologist was brought in and after testing Sarah she suggested enrolling her at a special correspondence school which has a programme of work that pupils do at home and then send in for marking. Sarah really loved it; she wrote a novel and still had time to indulge her passion for music and ballet. She danced in three full-length ballets and loved both classical and jazz ballet.

When she was four-and-a-half years old she started her first music lessons. Her parents bought her a box violin, which she instantly rejected, hardly giving it a glance. 'She wanted a real violin,' said Carol, and they found her a teacher called Sophie. After her first lesson Sarah said, 'I love Sophie, I love music, but most of all I love the violin.' When Sophie decided to give up teaching, another Irish woman like herself, Sabine Goor (a good old Irish name), took over and she immediately recognised Sarah's extraordinary talent. It was Sabine who suggested that they send a tape of Sarah's playing to the Yehudi Menuhin School. She was accepted as a pupil by the school, and six months later, after much persuasion, the McCrackens agreed to send her.

When she reached eight years of age Sarah made the long journey to England and started at her new school. The Yehudi Menuhin School, nestling at the edge of the beautiful Surrey countryside, caters for musically gifted children between the ages of eight and eighteen. Donations and gifts have enabled it to grow and it can now provide places for fifty students from countries all over the world, including Russia, Korea, Japan, France and, of course, New Zealand. The dream of Yehudi Menuhin and his life-long friend and colleague, Marcel Gazelle, has been realised in this establishment. Travelling the world for thirty years, this man of vision became painfully aware of the difficulties children face when studying music and having to cope with a normal school routine. The school provides not only expert tuition in stringed instruments and piano, but has a highly qualified staff teaching normal academic subjects. It was interesting to learn that English as a second language features amongst its wide-ranging language courses. Mr Chisolm kindly sent me the school's illustrated brochure, and I could not but envy the students their beautiful sunlit music rooms and classrooms – a far cry from the miserable, cheerless rooms of the boarding school I attended.

Carol McCracken says that Sarah is always busy, very innovative and imaginative in all she does; she prefers to play with children who are three years older than she is. She is quite concerned with fairness towards others, which has caused problems from time to time. Sarah gets on well with bright children and very slow children, but not so well with those in between. Her friendships are deep and meaningful and she does not understand why children like to score off each other.

'Sarah is not a group person,' says her mother. 'If she is put in a group she always seems to end up as the leader.' At the school she is the youngest of her group of seven and yet appears to be their leader – leading them on occasion into all sorts of mischief. Her headmaster, Mr Chisolm, describes her as 'unusually outgoing and imaginative'.

Not sure of what the future holds for Sarah, her mother says, 'She will at least leave something behind. She stands out very quickly in a crowd and was born to achieve ... in what, only time will tell.'

The film *Little Man Tate* has now crossed the Atlantic and has sparked off much renewed media interest in gifted children. I telephoned the British Mensa office in Wolverhampton to find out the name of the youngest member of British Mensa (which includes Irish Mensa); it was Katherine Barnes, aged three years nine months. When I rang her parents they told me that Katherine had accompanied her bright six-year-old brother to an educational psychologist for a testing session. The psychologist tested both the children (at Katherine's insistence) and her score was within the top one per cent for the test. Her interests are computer chess, museums, reading and mathematics. I asked her mother if she knew that Katherine was, apparently, the youngest member in the British Isles. 'No, I didn't,' she replied.

Four or five days later I spoke on the telephone to Harold Gale at the office in Wolverhampton. He had been inundated with press and television enquiries; all the national newspapers carried the 'Katherine' story. However, Harold informed me that in the few days which had passed since I had received the information about Katherine, it had become out of date; she was no longer the youngest member – Arin Bhalsod was younger by eleven days.

Replacing the receiver I switched on the lunch-time news; Katherine's story was one of the headlines on the BBC Television's national news. They ran an interview with the little girl and her mother. The sweet-faced child quietly answered the questions put to her, and it became apparent that she is going to need every bit of her inventive genius to attain her ambition in life – to become a mermaid!

I asked Harold Gale why, if they did not want to encourage publicity for these Mensa tots, they told the media about them. 'We don't,' he answered. 'We advise parents for the children's sake *not* to give media interviews.' I then realised that I was probably partly responsible for the news coverage, because I had informed Katherine's parents that she was Mensa's youngest member. I therefore beat a hasty retreat. As Harold said goodbye he told me that Arin Bhalsod would be appearing on Independent Television's 'Breakfast show' the following morning.

I am not one of the world's earliest risers (my head rarely hits the pillow before 1 a.m.); nevertheless, with great devotion to Mensa I dragged myself out of bed in the early hours of the next day to see and hear this little boy. It was not difficult to see from whom the gorgeous, alert child had inherited his looks. His attractive mother answered most of the questions as Arin examined the television monitors and gave a running commentary on who was on the screen – totally upstaging the amused lady presenter. He seemed delighted that he would not be going to school for the rest of the day and was as outgoing and natural as a child could be. I waited two days before telephoning his parents to get some more information about Arin.

'I'm going to buy a computer this afternoon,' said a chirpy voice. 'Who are you?' it asked, and I recognised Arin's rushed tones from my glimpse of him on television. Then Mrs Bhalsod came on the line; she was reluctant to talk to me at first but when I had convinced her that my call was genuine, she explained her wariness about exploiting Arin's giftedness. They were anxious to keep him absolutely natural and said that he had already forgotten the TV appearance. He was more advanced than most children of his own age and many of her friends had convinced her that she should approach Mensa to have him tested. Mensa in turn put her in touch with the Mensa Foundation for Gifted Children (MFGC). 'He is interested in exploring things around him and is very good with his hands,' his mother said, adding that he had a short attention span and was really excited at the prospect of owning a computer. This I gathered, as I could hear a piping little voice in the background urging her to hurry up! He really was a case of brains and beauty and, before being dragged off to the computer shop, his mother said, 'He does do some modelling.'

The press deluged the Irish Mensa office with enquiries following the TV appearance of these two children. David was taken aback by a call from the mother of a twenty-one-month-old, who informed him that her child was reading newspapers and could, after hearing any song twice, sing and remember every word. This little girl had perfect recall of incidents which happened nine months previously. 'Is she gifted?' her mother enquired. David referred her to MFGC but is still not sure if the child is gifted or if the mother has an amazing imagination.

Mensa as a society is reluctant to encourage very young children. They feel that there is little to offer them and fear that exploitation and pressure can, in some cases, do more harm than good. The testing of children under the age of six is carried out by psychologists and then, providing the stringent standard is achieved, the children can apply for membership.

Several of the children remarked that they would like to have their own magazine. Well, no sooner said than done. They now have their own journal, *Bright Sparks* edited by Aeon McNulty, and it fills a great need for those young enquiring minds. The children will be the major contributors.

The talent of these gifted children is obvious as soon as one reads their stories in the various SIG newsletters. A series of three poems about a fox was written by eleven-year-old Jacob Nevins. This one was my choice:

The dustbin fox

I wake up to the noise of cars
The smells of food, the clinks of jars
In metal trolleys, the blare of a horn
The murmur of people talking: dawn
Has long since passed.
The hypermarket
(For that is where I am: I see it)
Teems with people and people mean trouble.
Women walk round, and men with stubbled
Faces: I wish I was back in my den.
Far away a clock chimes ten.
I tensely lie nibbling an orange,
Waiting till nightfall, on the fringe
Of sleep.
Eventually darkness comes:

Floodlights glare; the building becomes
A sea of light.
I look out
On to the road; then I doubt
My vision; because I see
A familiar sight; trees
I jump out of the skip,
Ignoring the pain in my hip,
I run across the road: a lorry
Misses me by inches; worry
Pushes me onto the island,
I just manage to reach the woodland.
Looking around,
I find it is small,
I span the road, away from the mall.
A fog rolls over; coldness grips
Everything; the smell of chips
Lures me to a couple of bins;
Foraging in the full up tins
Gives me a meal of greasy fish
And the wrappers; gooey squish.
Satisfied, I jump into a garden;
But this night; the cold frost hardens
Everything from grass to flower
Hearing a car, I stop and cower
Behind a bush until it disappears.
When I come out a garden gnome leers
From a pond; I take a drink.
In the next garden the dustbin stinks.
In the one after I smell no man,
Knocking my paw on an old tin can,
Running along I come to a shed,
Finding a mouse, long since dead.
This is the perfect garden for a fox.
Morning comes, and I curl up on a box.
The last thing I hear is a woodpecker's knocks.

'I had just over a week to prepare *Pigasus* for publication,' David Riley said. The Special Interest Group newsletter urged members to write, so David penned a letter to Lynn Allcock and to the editorial board, pointing out the several changes that he would like to see and suggesting that the inclusion of a guest editor from time to time be considered. Lynn accepted the challenge and informed him that the contributions for the following edition were winging their way to him. 'I was a bit critical,' David admitted, 'but that's me. By the time I had posted the letter I had regretted what I had said.' Despite David's regrets, he quickly settled down to the task in hand. 'There wasn't much editing to do. Most of the material was published.' His greatest interest is computers. He set it up on his word processor, using the latest features, bold titles, headers and footers (designs or features at the top and bottom of the pages for those still using pen and ink, or a 'Bulldog Drummond' rubber stamp kit).

After a fortnight the printed magazine arrived. David was a little disappointed. 'The Mensa photocopier had gone on strike,' he said, 'cutting off the tops and bottoms of some pages, and an odd paragraph or two contained some unscheduled black lines. It was an enjoyable experience and it allowed me to take control of the newsletter. My next job in *Pigasus* was writing letters defending myself as editor!' said fifteen-year-old David.

'I abhor pop music,' Derek Hutcheson asserted. This fourteen-year-old former chorister achieved the award of the Royal School of Church Music, St Andrews, the highest award available to choristers in Scotland. His interest in church music continues but, when his voice broke, his days as a chorister came to an end.

Derek attends the largest private school in Scotland and is studying science, languages, mathematics and history. He is very musical and his interests are many and varied. Music is his first love, followed by motor sports, archaeology, painting and genealogy. Sport, he admits, is not high on his list of priorities but he plays tennis and, while confessing to being a beginner, he is, in his opinion (if nobody else's), improving. He has been a member of Mensa for two years and has become involved with the society. 'I seem to become involved in everything,' Derek said. He was introduced to Mensa by a competition which appeared on

Independent Television's teletext service, ORACLE. He successfully completed the competition, a self-administered home test, and was advised, on the strength of his result, to take the matter further, which he did.

Derek's interest in journalism has prompted him to contribute to several of the Mensa magazines. He also contributes to several commercial publications. He suggests that young Mensans get together to organise meetings and events in their own areas. 'I set out to become involved with Mensa, instead of waiting for it to become involved with me.' Derek Hutcheson is a name to watch.

One Saturday I answered the telephone and an agitated voice asked to speak to David. Well used to Saturday callers (testing sessions are held in Dublin on a Saturday), I explained that he was not available and I offered my assistance instead. The caller did not identify herself and asked if it would be possible to speak to him later that evening, it was about Mensa she said and it was urgent. I informed her he would not be available until Sunday evening and, hearing the urgency in her tone, repeated my offer of help.

'I want to leave Mensa,' she said tersely. 'I don't want my teachers or my school friends to find out that I belong to an élite society like Mensa.' This was no run-of-the-mill Saturday telephone call! 'I want to be taken off the list immediately,' she added. I confess that no answer sprang to my lips. She continued by asking if it would be possible to have a certificate before her name was removed from the register. I told her I did not know what the procedure was in such a case and asked her why she felt she should have some proof of membership if, indeed, she was so ashamed of being a member?

'I don't believe in élitism. I feel all people should be equal and the fact that not everyone can belong to Mensa is my reason for wanting to leave.' Somehow her voice seemed to lack conviction. I told her that she would have to contact David, and could not resist asking why she wanted a certificate, particularly as all members are issued with a membership card. 'I am applying for a special course being held in America which involves a sizeable grant, and being a member of Mensa would qualify me as an applicant.' My splutterings could be heard a long way off and, to the best of my knowledge, she has not been in touch with the offices since that time.

Someone who is rapidly making a name for himself is Fergal Breen, Ireland's nineteen-year-old Young Mensa officer. Naming himself the 'New Star Sheriff in Town' and 'Captain Mensa', he engaged in a country-wide tour but confessed he was disappointed at meeting fewer than one hundred Young Mensans. Promising to galvanise apathetic Young Mensans into action he intends to make a video film with, for and about Mensa and to introduce a new image into Irish Young Mensa.

Somewhere along the line the Junior Mensans become Young Mensans or, to be correct, they belong to the Young Mensa Special Interest Group (YMSIG). Originally this group was for members between the ages of sixteen and twenty-five, but such is the popularity of and interest in YM that now the youngest member is just over three years old and the older members (all lying unashamedly, I suspect) well above the proposed age limit.

The YMSIG and the bi-monthly newsletter are administered by Caroline Thaung, the newsletter written mostly by Young Mensans. Many of the members of this SIG are students studying in either schools or universities, but there are others in more diverse fields such as the Inland Revenue, fish farming, film making, modelling and the military. Events to enable young people to get together are organised and they cover many different activities and sound most interesting (yet another reason why I wish I were twenty-one again, and again, and again, and again).

One particular weekend included a talk by Terry Pratchett, an author who is enormously popular throughout Mensa with young and old alike, a visit to the Stewart Crystal Factory to watch the manufacture and engraving of their famous glass and a midnight beach party.

Caroline, despite embarking on a career as a doctor, took a year out of her medical studies to earn a degree in psychology. Her interests, when her busy schedule permits, include Tai Chi Chu'an, play-by-mail games, piano playing, ballroom dancing and tearing around on a motor bike.

She is a Mensa test supervisor, and is careful to emphasise that Young Mensa is not a society of eggheads, Tefal men and top-secret research scientists. At one meeting there was a new member who was introduced to everyone and thoroughly enjoyed the evening. After the gathering he told Caroline how nice and how 'non-eggheaded' everyone had been. He had spent time chatting to a pleasant young couple and asked what they did for a living. Caroline reluctantly informed him they were nuclear physicists!

'What is noisy and wet, with 238 legs?' asked Neil Goulder, British Mensa's Treasurer, among many other things. (Most people, after seeing his surname in writing, mispronounce it; he usually tells them that it rhymes with a section of his anatomy. You lateral thinkers can work it out – a clue: it isn't ankle.) Without the aid of a calculator, and trying to outguess Neil Elbow (getting warmer, now) my answer is 119 Young Mensans.

Neil advertised a weekend at the Center Parcs leisure centre (that's my spelling and I'm sticking to it) and was bowled over by the response. The accommodation, which consisted entirely of villas, was booked a year in advance and, when all the available places had been filled, there were still 200 clamouring Young Mensans on the waiting list. The leisure centre is situated in the heart of Sherwood Forest and focuses on sport. The first of the sporting activities began on Friday evening in the cocktail bar. The aim? To sample everything on the menu, paper umbrellas and all. A games inventor, Jeremy Shaw, gave the group an insight into the games industry and introduced his own game, 'Trinity', the rules of which were deceptively simple but the strategy elusive. The lanes of the bowling alley were buzzing with Mensans as latecomers joined the throng, and when the hour of bowling ended they followed their ears to the disco.

Bed time? Not likely. Party time? Definitely. The groups in their villas partied until the early hours and still managed to arrive at the crack of dawn for the 11 a.m. aerobics session. A couple of hours' skill testing were divided between badminton, roller skating and – this *was* Sherwood Forest – archery.

The centrepiece of the complex is an enormous domed building containing the most imaginative water attractions. The energetic swam in the magnificent pool with its tropical plants, battled with machine-powered waves, whooshed down tubular slides and shot the rapids. Synchronised drowning was of course a feature and they found an able demonstrator of the art in Clare Jenner. The prune-skinned group then treated themselves to two huge tubs of ice cream and retired to one of the villas to celebrate.

On Saturday evenings Center Parcs organise a dinner dance and Neil said, 'The manageress remembered me from the previous year.' (Surprise! surprise!) Despite this, the best tables were reserved for the eighty-strong group, many of whom were in fancy dress. Other guests appeared to enjoy the antics of these exuberant dancers and the night ended with a huge villa party and marshmallow cremation (fortunately, not the other way around).

Sunday was a more leisurely day. The Mensan Center Parcs Classic Open was held on the mini-golf course. A toga party, followed by a disco party, followed by a villa party brought the proceedings to a close. The question most asked the following morning was, 'Can I book now for next year?'

Neil, it is whispered, is one of those Young Mensans who refuses to relinquish membership of the group, although rumoured to be approaching his dotage, and there is a distinct possibility that in the future Young Mensa will only accept members between the ages of one and a hundred.

One Young Mensan repeated an incident or, I should say, yet another incident, involving Mensans stuck in lifts. It appears that at a recent annual gathering a group of YMs were about to close the doors of a lift when two extra figures appeared and squashed into the lift which started its ascent and then ground to a noisy halt between two floors; there were more people on board than the lift was meant to carry. Eventually the doors were half-opened disgorging the two culprits, David and our daughter Lynda. Immediately after their exit the doors slammed shut with enough force to decapitate. Lynda has a dislike of lifts which started when, as a tiny child, she and David were trapped in one due to a power failure in a hotel in Italy. The two of them sat on the floor of the darkened box and, anxious to reassure her, David explained that the lights would come on again quite soon. To keep her calm he sang nursery rhymes and told her to join in. After about five minutes the power returned, by which time the concerned and kindly hotel owners were gathered around the lift doors (together with the expert worrier, me). Soothing and fussing over the child, the paternal owner asked, 'Were you afraid, Lynda?' 'Not until my Daddy started to sing!' she replied.

These bright young revellers enjoy their get-togethers and charitable works are very much a part of their activities. They can be found taking part in home-made raft races, pushing hospital beds along streets, marathon running, parachute jumping, hang gliding and, on the more cerebral side, competing in pub quizzes.

The Young Mensans may project a hedonistic image but, in fact, many of them are immersed in their studies at universities and other seats of learning, or are making their names in the workplace or earning high honours in schools. Tomorrow's generation is not afraid to claim its rightful place in the world of Mensa.

CHAPTER 8

Special Interest Groups

'Is anyone in Mensa interested in high-flying, low-powered lawn mowers?' 'Probably.' 'Is there a Special Interest Group on the subject?' 'There will be when you start one.' This may be a slight exaggeration as to content, but it is true as to the way many of the SIGs (Special Interest Groups) are created. Hair-tearing SIGSecs (editors) across the land struggle to meet their self-imposed deadlines and produce their newsletters on time.

Within British Mensa there are over eighty-five active SIGs, each with a newsletter, some appearing monthly, others as infrequently as once a year. Members of British and Irish Mensa are entitled to belong to two SIGs without charge. They may, of course, join any other SIGs which interest them for a small fee to cover photocopying, postage and office expenses.

I called up Wolverhampton to ask if they would send me a few samples of SIG newsletters as I wanted to get an idea of their subject matter, writers, size, etc. Three days later, when I was confined to bed with influenza, the parcel arrived. A large box, which almost broke my legs, was placed on the bed; it contained at least two copies of each newsletter and an alphabetically listed index to guide me. My time of enforced rest would not be wasted. One month later, with my legs healing nicely thank you, I reached the bottom of the pile for the second time; somewhere along the way I had lost my ability to 'skip-read'.

'Miaow,' said the cover of what was undoubtedly the most copiously illustrated of the newsletters. There was hardly one of the thirty-two pages of feline news which did not bear some form of drawing, cartoon or picture of the fluffy creatures. On the back cover of one issue was a cartoon of two half-hidden cats seated contentedly with their paws up in comfortable armchairs, in front of them a television set, between them a table on which was placed a large bowl of popcorn and a well-filleted fish skeleton. The caption: 'I just love it when they go away for the whole weekend!' This was the work of Rosalie Moscovitch of Canadian Mensa. 'Catney and Lacey' and 'Paws for thought' were feature articles. Venues and dates of cat shows throughout Britain and Ireland, poems, jewellery and 'Miaow' tee-shirts were on offer to the newsletter's devoted readers.

Maureen Day, the SIG's secretary and editor, has many varied interests: investment clubs, walking, shopping, detective stories and, needless to say, cats. She is a tax inspector by profession and says she has not found herself too unpopular. At one stage there she found herself attending meetings along with a VAT inspector.

Mark Griffin is the head honcho of these groups or, to give him his full and correct title, Special Interest Groups Officer. Mark is into SIGs in a big way. When he joined Mensa he wrote to seventeen of the groups and joined twelve. 'Seeing the effort that many of the hard-working SIG secs put into their groups is what motivates me in my role of SIGs officer,' he says. Mark is a Cray supercomputer engineer, which, he told me, does not mean that he is a super computer engineer (what a difference a space makes!). These vast computers are at the top of the pecking order in terms of power and complexity.

Mark guides the busy SIG secretaries and editors and helps them with their difficulties and queries. He also deals with any problems sent in by members and contributors. He keeps a watchful eye on the material published in the newsletters; any form of discrimination, racism, bigotry or vicious personal attack would result in the offending newsletter immediately being closed down. Prejudices of this nature have no place in Mensa and I am reliably informed that they rarely occur. He publicises the various groups within Mensa and writes a monthly column for the *Mensa Magazine*.

'SUSY and the WIMP'. Is this a story of unrequited love perhaps? No, it was the title of an article in not one but two of the newsletters. Delving further I discovered that SUSY is not one of Mensa's unstretched lady members but part of the 'supersymmetry' theories with which the physicists are having a problem – doesn't everybody? The WIMP? You guessed – something equally obscure in the eye of the space-uninitiated; it is a weakly interacting massive particle.

The SIG sec. himself, Colin Wagstaff, is the author of this and many other articles in *Spacesignal*, a journal for those who are interested in space in its various forms. An article by a Russian cosmonaut, head of the cosmonaut training programme, explaining the mode of transferring from one orbital space station to another, flare stars, the sun and 'ET go home', are other items which filled the twenty-eight-page newsletter and which will need more careful reading on my part before the complexities of space blast off in my brain.

Included in every newsletter is a statement to the effect that 'all opinions expressed are those of individual contributors. Mensa as an organisation has no opinions.'

Singles is the largest SIG with well over 1,000 members. That is not its only claim to fame; it is probably the only group that is happy when its membership is reduced because its participants have met, married and become ineligible. There are members who have joined Mensa because they had heard of this SIG.

Laurie Bredbury, team leader of the newsletter, and I have become good friends, despite my attempts to ruin his life. Keen to get information and opinions from the cool editor of this singles group, I telephoned him at home. 'May I ask you some questions?' 'You may,' came the polite reply, 'but not now.' The time was 9.30 p.m. and he was heading off to bed. I tried again the following evening and sneakily enquired if he had an early start to his day. It transpired that he had enjoyed a very full weekend. Laurie enjoys a social life second to none and that was the reason for his early retirement the previous night. He was friendly and extremely helpful and told me that if I needed any further information not to hesitate to contact him. I did call again. 'You don't half pick your moments,' the cheerful voice informed me, 'I have a large plate of chicken curry steaming here.' I rang off immediately with instructions to try again half an hour later.

The subject of this call was a poem that had attracted my attention in the newsletter and Laurie, with good-natured swiftness, found me the telephone number of the poetess concerned, Jean Hayes. Jean was a delight to talk to, cheerful, friendly and full of the joys of spring. Her four children are now grown up and she is living life to the full. She has been a member of Mensa for two years and because of it she has met many people, found new interests, taken up new hobbies. She is a piano teacher by profession and enjoys writing verse. One of her poems was recently published in the *Spectator*. In short, she is a busy lady.

Mischance

Twice have I loved immodestly
Though for the briefest span,
Inspired by youth's naïvety I found the perfect man,
On London's teeming underground
Approaching Leicester Square,
We pledged our souls in bliss profound
Across the moving stair.
Wild ecstasy soon wore a frown;
Starving, I could not sup
For he, alas, was going down
And I was coming up.

In middle age I scorned all men,
Passion deemed absurd,

So I was inattentive when
The second chance occurred.
One rush-hour night at Turnpike Lane,
Assuming no disguise,
My second love with message plain
Transfixed me with his eyes.
How full of bitterness the cup
That toasts a broken clown
For this time – he was going up
And I was coming down.

The editorial of the *Single* journal stressed that age does not matter; it is unimportant. People of all ages are members of the group. One of the singles, a gorgeous, sexy, lovable sweetheart, is a most popular person with over 100 people who send her a birthday card each year. She is fifty-six years old. The member who taught Laurie scuba diving is a man of sixty-five and the oldest member of this SIG lists his date of birth as 1900. Three engagements and two weddings are accredited to the SIG (eat your heart out, *Blind Date*). Members contact each other, outings are organised, holidays are planned – China, maybe? Eastern Europe? Blackpool? The social events are endless: in one month alone there were visits to the ballet, to a jazz club, to the cinema, a musical evening with the BBC Philharmonic Orchestra, the regular meeting, a sailors and sirens weekend, a dinner and a dinner dance, an outing for the day (happy to include children of single parents). It's no wonder that Laurie is in bed by 9.30 p.m.

Motorsig would appear to be self-explanatory. Not quite, its main concern is motor cycles, but now a car SIG has just been born. Peter Brooke is its SIGSec. and he wrote to tell me about it. Adding his good wishes for the book, he expressed the hope that the contents would be better than the title!

Flypaper continues the transport theme and if you are an up-up-and-awayer this is the one for you. One enthusiastic member turned part of his farm into a landing strip and held a weekend fly-in. He has now bulldozed a longer strip and the fly-in could become a regular feature on the SIG's calendar (which members of the caravan SIG may join). The newsletter covers all aspects of flying, including parachute jumping; no subscription to this worthy journal will be winging its way to the devoted SIG sec. from me.

For the energetic there are *Rambling and Mountaineering* and *Dig* (not the mountains, the garden). Keen ramblers and climbers can indulge their taste not only for exercise but also for good company. One of the SIG's members claims that he found soul mates for the first time in his life and he added that for this alone he felt deeply indebted to Mensa. The copy of *Dig* that was included in the enormous pile of information was a supplement containing a concise monthly guide to gardening chores; reading it gave my guilty conscience a gentle tug – which I chose to ignore.

Soccer enthusiasts are not forgotten. Their journal is packed with information, quizzes and puzzles on every aspects of the game. For those who are knowledgeable about the sport this is a very entertaining SIG.

Home from the hills and with the garden ready for public viewing day, rosy-cheeked Mensans take to their armchairs with food for thought. Every interest is catered for: philosophy, poetry, the occult, life enhancement, astrology, religion, politics, writing, history, genealogy, health and fitness – to name but a few.

'Dear friends' is the commonest form of greeting in *M-to-M*, the SIG newsletter for members isolated geographically or by circumstance. Reading it was like peeping into the lives of a group of friends gathered together in order to catch up with each other's news. Carrie Howse, the SIGSec., is obviously regarded with affection by her flock. One letter, written in beautiful Gothic-style script, humorously described a member's holidays and his son's wedding. The words and writing flowed until he reached the stage where he wanted to give a report on the bride's dress; here, the writing became a little smaller as he added his ex-wife's expert fashion report.

Darlings, luvies, if you love dramatic art Madsoc is the SIG for you. As the name suggests, if you are just a teensie bit mad that's a bonus. Jill Pimblett (clad in pantomime costume, she confided over the telephone), the bubbly, fun-loving, out-going actress, was full of enthusiasm for the art and the SIG newsletter she edits. Many of the shyer contributors to the newsletter confessed a preference for staying in the wings. Others reported on the various parts they were playing either professionally or in amateur drama groups. One critic-cum-stage-manager-cum-prompter gave his humorous account of a nightmarish week in the theatre with a production of *Blithe Spirit*, involving broken limbs, collapsing scenery and temperamental actors. An enthusiastic letter from Jill described a weekend that some members of the SIG had recently enjoyed. It comprised acting, improvisations, workshops and theatre visits. A prize for the best characterisation was on offer and the group descended on a local restaurant 'in character'. A non-English-speaking 'Russian' thespian gave such a convincing performance that a sympathetic waitress gave Jill a huge handful of chocolate mints 'for the Russian 'cos he won't get chocolate over there'! The thank-you letters from Jill's guests left the reader in no doubt as to the enjoyment of the weekend – a marvellous bloodshot couple of days. How about a Mensa pantomime and, seeing that Mensans would be involved, why not in the middle of summer? Or would that be a teensie bit mad?

The SIG newsletters based on television programmes such as *Monty Python* and *Star Trek* have their cult following in both Britain and the US, as have those based on comic-strip characters. Music has no fewer than three journals, and the arts SIG newsletter encourages views on anything from sculpture to classic films.

The humour SIG newsletter, with its jokes and stories, has a large fan club. Cartoons feature largely, plays have their place of honour and one number contained a very clever drawing. It showed a pretty girl, and the caption was, 'Before marriage'. When it was turned upside-down the pretty girl became an ugly crone and, you guessed it, 'After marriage' was the caption.

Computers, business interests, design, inventions, travel and naturally, this being Mensa, quizzes and puzzles are well represented. *Green Scene* and *Animal Rights* prove that Mensans are concerned about the environment and animals. *Linguasig*, with its seventy-six pages, clocks in as the bulkiest of the newsletters. A useful guide to the 100 most-used words was translated into French, Italian, Spanish, Swedish, Japanese, Chinese and Esperanto.

ThYMe is the SIG with the next-to-largest membership – about 1,000 members. It aims to put Young Mensans from all over the world in touch with one another. Ages range from three years to twenty-six and Caroline Thaung, the SIG sec., has, I suspect, a difficult time getting her 'elderly chicks' to leave the nest. Members of ThYMe write the newsletter's articles, stories and puzzles. Caroline has been a member of the British Mensa committee and a NatRep on the International Board of Directors. She is studying medicine in Glasgow and, despite her busy social life, still has time for ThYMe.

'Spreading the word' has acquired a whole new meaning in our house. Hundreds of thousands of words contained in these SIG newsletters are spread on every conceivable surface vying for attention. These journals are not the only form of communication for the SIG members; many of them meet socially to share their common interests and are encouraged to do so both formally and informally. One letter expressed delight at the possibility of at last being able to 'find another weird and wonderful person such as I', and several letters echoed this.

Mensans are not what you might call straightforward. Take the case of the SIG of British Mensa which offers help to those who wish to learn more about the German language, couple that with German Mensa's SIG for those keen to add French and Spanish to their linguistic abilities. Observe that Spanish Mensa offers an Esperanto SIG, while Mensa Austria has leanings towards an English-speaking SIG. Then, to complicate matters, realise that Dutch Mensa has a bi-lingual SIG for those with a yen for Spanish culture. That is quite enough of that.

Having read the previous paragraph you could not be blamed for rushing to join the SUP SIG, the Society for Upgrading Plonk. Despite its unpretentious title, this newsletter is extremely knowledgeable and some of the 'plonk' discussed could be justifiably hurt by the description. Wine tastings, usually accompanied with, or followed by, food give its members the opportunity to test many of the wines, champagnes and malts. Suggestions of travel abroad are mooted for the devotees of the gentle art of elbow raising.

The SIGs of American Mensa are mind-boggling in their variety; there are almost 200 of them, I am informed. The interests of their 55,000 members would fill a large volume. Many of the SIGs are common to all the national Mensas, particularly Young Mensa and the Gifted

Children. Others are shared across the great Atlantic Ocean.

I will not beat about the bush, the Chocoholics SIG would prove impossible to resist if we lived in the United States. The mammoth bars of multi-coloured chocolate provided by the SIG at the regional gathering in Philadelphia were a great temptation. Chopping off a piece of the chocolate with a miniature cleaver, I remarked to David that I preferred the ordinary-coloured chocolate. The grins on the faces of David and the people standing beside him made me realise that with my brilliant sense of colour I had done it again; the chocolate I had eaten was red. The aim of the SIG is to discover the connection between high intelligence and all things chocolate. Hear, hear!

The 'three As' of the American Mensa SIGs are groups which offer much-needed support and help to sufferers and carers alike. Alkafriends deals with the problems of alcoholics. Alzheimer's disease and other senile dementias are discussed, experiences shared and informal counselling offered in respect of this very distressing affliction. Adoption is the third of the help groups; it was upsetting to learn that 100,000 children in the US are in need of homes.

'Three trillion Mensans own, or are involved with, computers,' says International Director, Ed Vincent. Not content with one computer SIG newsletter, American Mensa has four, *Amstrad PCW Users' Group*, *Apple Computer* and *Macintosh*. Should any of the directors of these companies wish to thank me for the publicity, I can be reached c/o Mensa Publications; there will be someone there to accept delivery – deliveries! The fourth SIG, Computer Hobbyists, is equally important but membership does not involve allegiance to one brand of computer.

Mystery Book Swap offers its members – a mystery-book swap. Two mysteries in fact. Send two, receive two is the simple and much-appreciated formula. As book prices soar daily this is a very sensible method of acquiring and disposing of reading matter.

There is a food SIG on the huge American list. It is surprising that there is no food SIG in British Mensa, but I will say no more in case I get roped in to start one. Members of the food SIG share recipes, ideas and the joys of cooking through their newsletter. *Oriental Cooking* has the same aims but adds a hard-to-find service for food items. Vegetarians are not forgotten and their newsletter, *Vegetarian Life*, deals with all aspects of healthy living, food, philosophy and prints personal stories.

The lazy, listless, lackadaisical, lollygagging, languid loafers finally got around to setting up a Procrastinators' SIG and they invite you to join them. Their newsletter is semi-annual.

A recent article by Mark Griffin in the *Mensa Magazine* tells of a visit an American procrastinators' club made to London. (How did they manage to organise that trip?) They went to the Whitechapel Foundry to make a claim on the two-hundred-year guarantee which had been issued with the Liberty Bell. Cast in 1752 the bell cracked in 1835. Despite the fact that the guarantee had run out, this much-respected firm decided to honour the guarantee. All the Americans had to do was to return the bell, in its original packing, and they would receive the full refund of £60. There was no confirmation available as to whether the visitors had any connection to the American Mensa SIG.

Gold and Creative retirement are two groups for Mensa members who are supposed to be enjoying leisurely days, but knowing Mensans, they are probably busier at this stage of their lives than ever before. This has certainly proved to be the case for the many Mensans I have spoken to or, more correctly, those I have managed to contact. It has not been an easy task. Forget the old adage, 'life begins at forty', sixty would be a more accurate starting figure for these retirees. Consultancies, book authorship, travel and hobbies keep these elusive members on the go twenty-five hours a day.

Most SIGSecs welcome membership from other countries and it is not difficult to find a SIG with members from far-off lands. This minute glimpse does not do justice to the talent, mental agility, physical mobility, sexual virility and creative ability of members of the Special Interest Groups throughout the world of Mensa.

CHAPTER 9

Getting it together

For some Mensans the most satisfying part of their membership is found in debate, discussion and argument. They are proud of their high IQ and make no apology for their cultural, intellectual, philosophical and linguistic abilities. Collectively, or individually, their knowledge in many areas is awe-inspiring but rarely are they condescending or patronising. There is little room in Mensa for swollen heads; they are firmly and swiftly reduced to shrunken heads. Pomposity is knocked on the head in double quick time. The most intelligent people ask for explanations when they do not understand a point or a fact and Mensa teaches one very quickly that to listen is to learn.

Many people do not enjoy the weekly or monthly pub meetings, jumping off bridges attached to a rope, cinema outings, picnics or even the larger, noisier gatherings. Their preference is for smaller groups and often, having met and matched minds, they arrange small get-togethers for quiet conversation in a congenial atmosphere. These can take place in a restaurant or private house and, over the years, have resulted in the formation of many long and lasting friendships.

For those who enjoy a more formal gathering there are the black-tie dinners of British Mensa. These dinners were originated by Roland Berrill, one of Mensa's founders, and Victor Serebriakoff has kept the tradition alive. He recalled the earlier dinners – Roland Berrill glaring at one of the diners and instructing him to propose a topic for discussion.

The dinners are 'mildly chaired' by Mensa's Honorary President, Victor Serebriakoff. Formal dress, black tie for the men and evening dresses for the ladies, in Victor's estimation raises the expectation of the evening.

A drink at the bar before dinner encourages conviviality, and at eight o'clock the 'guests' sit down to dine. 'It is most important that the tables are either square or round,' Victor explained. 'A long table encourages the conversation to break into groups.' Each of the diners introduces him or herself briefly and then four or five topics are proposed by the chair. Wine is served with the meal and this, no doubt, helps the more inhibited to enter the discussions.

Conversation flows, lively debate gets under way and Victor admitted that many a tired waiter has coughed discreetly behind his hand, drawing attention to the hour. A little penguin told me that the best seat at one of these dinners is between Victor and his wife Wyn, where one can listen to their witty sallies; neither gives any quarter to the other's views. People who enjoy the relaxed atmosphere and excellent conversation return again and again to these dinners.

Members of American Mensa seeking more serious debate than those offered by annual or regional gatherings welcomed the experimental introduction of the Annual Mensa Colloquium. The project, introduced in 1982, was the brainchild of Gabriel Werber (then Chairman of American Mensa). Since their inception the Colloquia have proved to be a popular addition to the cerebral programme of American Mensa. Spread over three days they focus, unlike the black-tie dinners, on just one subject. 'Forecasting a valid tomorrow: Destination AD 2000',

'The gifted in society', 'The impact of arts on civilisation', 'The politics of politics' have been some of the topics discussed.

The Colloquia are residential and usually commence on a Friday night. After registration, there is a welcoming reception and an introduction by a speaker who outlines the chosen theme. Trained facilitators (or moderators) conduct the groups which the following day, having been addressed by qualified and eminent speakers, take part in 'break-out' sessions. During these sessions the smaller groups discuss and debate the topic in detail; ideas and opinions abound and the atmosphere is informal and social. Hans Fromer, whom we had the pleasure of meeting in Dublin, was the treasurer for Colloquium VI, 'The politics of politics' held in Milwaukee. He explained that although there is a pattern to these Colloquia each one does have an individual approach. Saturday night cocktails and a banquet were, on this occasion, followed by a highly entertaining hour or so of political satire. Breakfast and a summary of the deliberations of the 'break-out' groups bring the weekend to a close. Each participant subsequently receives a summation of the Colloquium. One enthusiastic participant commented that the Colloquium is simply the most energising, mind-focusing event in Mensa.

Mensa at Cambridge (MAC) has been described as mind-stretching, an intellectual feast, brain food and, by one Canadian, Sylvie Oulette, as 'the best event I have ever attended'. Over a period of years the beautiful old colleges of Trinity, Queens' and, in 1992, Magdalene, have played host to delegates from all over the world, during six days of lectures, discussions, laughter, food, drink, education and discovery.

Year after year, during the first week in August, a certain number of Mensans return to MAC. It's a bit like a ritual or a migration. Why do they do this? It could only be for one of two reasons: A, they did not understand it the first time, or B, they liked it so much they just wanted to begin again. Sylvie decided it was B.

After attending five consecutive years, with each gathering lasting six days, Sylvie reckons that we can safely assume that she has been to MAC for thirty days. Curiously enough each of these thirty days have all been completely different.'

Every year a theme is chosen and invited lecturers speak on a related subject, but often end up talking about something entirely different.

Some of the delegates attend when the chosen topic suits them, others, however, couldn't care less. The reason for this is that there is more to MAC than lectures; there are conferences and social events, there are regulars and newcomers, barbecues and formal dinners. There are delegates from all over the planet.

No MAC gathering would be complete without punting expeditions on the Cam and, of course, it goes without saying that some end up in the river, either deliberately or not. 'This is one of the aspects that makes it all so charming,' Sylvie declared. Another constant is the fact that the weather is always pleasant. 'Those last few days of summer would really be enjoyable if the lectures were held outdoors. But', she added, 'that is just a minor detail. It does, however, rain occasionally – usually on bar-becue night!' This must be a 'Canuck' view of English weather.

There have been unique moments. A few years ago an eclipse of the moon was due to take place during the week (talk about organisation!). Many of the delegates ended up on the roof in the small hours of the morning in order to witness this event that had been especially planned for them. The skies were clear that night and soon everybody's atten-tion was grabbed by the sight of satellites gliding across the skies, till somebody pointed out that it was funny to see Mensans, who were supposedly watching the eclipse of the moon, with their backs turned at the critical time.

Another great occasion was a medieval banquet; all the diners dressed up and took a trip back in time. 'Eating with one's fingers', Sylvie observed, 'is not something one would want to do every night, especially when wearing a costume that has been hired, and there is a penalty charge for stains and rips.'

What more could I say about MAC? Quite a lot. Will the Canuck ever go back? You can bet her whole country on it. Somehow, some-thing keeps her going back for more – even though she always under-stands the first time.

Margaret Kavanagh (Clark), long-time treasurer of both British and International Mensa, remembers fondly many of the MAC gatherings. She said cries of 'Eureka' welcomed the speakers Ned Jago, inventor of the one-person submarine, and Wing Commander Wallis, inventor of the autogyro, as seen in a James Bond film. A life-sized model of each in the court at Queens' College made an interesting contrast to the college's Mathematical Bridge. Mensa, Margaret reflected, brings many diverse people together. Ned Jago had a deprived childhood, Wing Commander Wallis a comfortable one. Yet they both had keen, intelligent, inventive minds and their lectures made delightful and enlightening listening.

There were hilarious scenes when the University Theatre wardrobe opened for the MAC delegates to hire costumes for the medieval banquet. Americans, Australians, Canadians, Italians and many other nationalities were transformed into jesters, wizards, lords, ladies, scullions, beggars, food-tasters, etc. Many a manly leg was encased in tights and foot shod in curly-toed or buckled pumps. The serving staff also dressed in costume and a delicious meal of seven or eight courses was eaten with fingers or, at most, with a wooden spoon, and washed down with mead. Serenading went on in the minstrel gallery and the magnificent sixteenth-century hall was candlelit. A magical evening full of laughter.

The icebreaker, of course, plays a part at MAC as it does at all Mensa Gatherings. A Canadian Mensan, Tony Rowe, really broke the ice at one by playing pop songs on the piano in Old Hall. A member of a passing group of tourists, seeing the sign requesting silence for the conferences respectfully commented, 'That room is full of geniuses.' In Tig Warner's opinion, 'The icebreakers are hardly necessary, there's no ice to break.' Tig, unlike some of the delegates, does not hail from a far-off land; her home country is England, her home town, Cambridge.

Tig, who is one of the regulars, said that when she was faced with writing something about the intellectual side of MAC her immediate thought was 'What intellectual side? We all have so much fun that there isn't one.' Then, taking out her memorabilia, she recalled that in spite of spending all of one's time revelling and being happy, one can actually learn something about the subjects under discussion.

'Eureka', subtitled 'Inventing the future', was the theme of Tig's first visit to MAC. The legendary 'welcome to new members' was real, she observed. Though she enjoys the formal schedule of lectures and discussions, she says the less formal aspect is the reason 'for my returning year after year'.

'Getting through', 'Artificial intelligence', 'The leading edge', '20/20 vision', 'Space', 'Sex power and money', each theme or topic has its learned and renowned speakers. Discussions spill over from the conference and lecture halls into the hospitality rooms where the debates continue, aided by a little alcohol to soothe dry throats.

Mensa at Cambridge was introduced by Sir Clive Sinclair in 1980. It has been hailed over and over again as the number-one Mensa event. For many years the highlight of the six days has been the buffet party at Clive's beautiful house in Cambridge, with superb music playing in the background, food served on the lawn and not a rain drop in sight.

Dr Jack Cohen, a professor of biology and past Chairman of Mensa, praised the atmosphere, the company, the conversation. In his opinion MAC is an opportunity to meet and talk to interesting people and to enjoy good company in beautiful surroundings in an informal manner.

It has been difficult to find anybody who can remember the details of lectures, workshops and debates who does not start digressing about the formal and informal dinners, the punting on the Cam, the informal croquet tournament (which has never produced a winner), the friendships made and, to quote Dr Cohen, 'the good clean fun'.

One gentleman admitted to finding the lectures so soothing that he attended in order to have a good hour's sleep. A lady boasted proudly that she had never attended a single lecture on any of her many visits. Our daughter Lynda joined David at MAC and thoroughly enjoyed her 'six-day university education'. She introduced a lateral-thinking puzzle one evening. More and more people drifted over to help solve it, abandoning a disco which was taking place at the other end of the room. Lynda was not permitted to forget this for the rest of her stay.

'The essence of Mensa at Cambridge is that whilst it appears on the surface to be a formal conference there is much more to it than that,' Tig Warner observed. As the days pass people grow more relaxed; they realise they can talk without limiting their vocabulary, can crack obscure jokes without having to explain them. 'It is very special to find that anything not immediately understood is instantly queried; a level of communication seldom attained elsewhere is possible here.'

Mensa is about choices; there is within the society something for everyone if they wish to avail themselves of it. The shortest communication I received was from Ellin I. Selin, of Tulsa, Oklahoma and it stated simply: 'Mensa has filled my need for intellectual and mental nutrition. Its publications are brain food in the true sense.'

CHAPTER 10

Wedding bells

G iven the large number of single people in Mensa it is inevitable
that wedding bells will sound from time to time in the Mensa
world as couples meet and marry. Some have been known to
tie the knot at Mensa gatherings.

One such wedding was an intriguing item on the programme of the
American Mensa annual gathering in Atlanta, Georgia. David joined the
smartly dressed crowd in the beautifully decorated inner courtyard of
the Radisson Hotel where a modern-day Rhett and Scarlett were preparing to plight their troth to each other in the company of their
Mensa family. Nancy Fitch and Oscar Zeigler were the bride and groom
and the ceremony was performed by another Mensan. An odd tear here
and there was hastily wiped away with a flash of a Kleenex and several
other Mensa couples renewed their vows. The reception was held in a

hospitality suite and everyone present enthusiastically participated in a thoroughly enjoyable afternoon.

There are no figures available of how many Mensans are married to Mensans, but I am sure that it would not be an exaggeration to say thousands worldwide. Carrie Ann Nielsen and Paul Cantwell are the first Irish Mensa couple that we know who met and married through Mensa. Unfortunately we were unable to attend their wedding but we know they are living happily ever after. We know of several other Irish Mensans who met their future spouses at Mensa Annual Gatherings, and it would be interesting to discover how many couples had met through Mensa, and how many married couples had joined.

A letter listing ten separate items arrived from South Carolina. D. Paul Somerville generously offered to supply details of any or all of them: meetings, experiences, travelling and attending Mensa weddings abroad. I chose the weddings and the armchair travelling. (Oh! The power of it all.)

Paul describes himself as suffering from terminal wanderlust. During his first year as a Mensan he attended gatherings in nine countries but, instead of that satisfying his itchy feet, it merely whetted his appetite for more. 'I could not wait to become part of an organisation that would instantly extend to me the hospitality of countries around the globe,' he said.

Paul's wanderlust became apparent as I read that he is a graduate of Duke University, North Carolina; he resides in South Carolina and is the local secretary of the Savannah, Georgia Mensa group. He joined Mensa in 1986 when 'much of the world was still surrounded by the iron curtain of communism'. Coincidentally it was also the year that we met him at the Ruby Anniversary gathering in Oxford.

Anxious to bridge the East–West understanding gap he contacted the International Office and obtained the names and addresses of two Mensans in Poland, Tomek Berent of Lodz and Edward Waslewicz of Sportowa near Wroclaw. A prolific correspondence began. They were eager to explore each other's world and the opportunity for Paul to do so arose when an invitation to attend Edward's forthcoming wedding arrived. 'I was ecstatic,' said Paul.

At first the logistics of the journey seemed insurmountable. Which airline? Would he obtain a visa? Could he take the time off work? What would he wear for the wedding in view of the intense cold he knew he must expect there? Come what may, he had made up his mind to go. With tickets booked, visa in order and Edward's promise to meet him at Warsaw Airport it was all systems go.

He landed in Warsaw on a bitterly cold November day and was immediately impressed by the invasive presence of Polish and Soviet soldiers armed with menacing AK-47s. Paul laboured his way through the bureaucratic maze, which included buying $15-worth of Polish zlotys for each day of his stay. Ruefully he later realised that the official rate of exchange was only one-fifth of that available from the street-corner 'bankers'.

At last the pen friends met for the first time. Edward could best be described as dashing. A square jaw, Omar-Sharif eyes, a dark flowing pelisse and Cossack hat instantly conjured up visions of Dr Zhivago. Edward's train journey from Wroclaw to Warsaw had taken eight long, freezing-cold hours. 'Where outside Mensa could you find such kindness?' Paul wondered.

The two men went by taxi to a Warsaw restaurant. Edward apologised for his poor English which, he said, was his fourth language; Paul described it as excellent. Their meal of bortsch (beetroot soup), cabbage and beef with beets was enjoyable, but everywhere Paul turned he saw armed and watchful soldiers. It was obvious to all that Edward had a foreigner in tow.

Next came the eight-hour train ride to Wroclaw.

Their fellow passengers recognised Paul as an American and went out of their way to be friendly and hospitable. That set the tone for the whole of his trip. What made the strongest impression on that journey were the barren landscapes and endless series of small villages, all covered with a layer of dingy soot, and Paul was struck by the startling contrast between Eastern Europe's Olympic excellence, advanced military technology and deplorable environmental circumstances. It soon became all too apparent what had been sacrificed for military technology.

A five-star hotel in Wroclaw would not have earned five stars in the West, but it was more than adequate for Paul's needs and it had all been arranged and paid for in advance by Edward, Malgorzata, Edward's bride-to-be, and their respective families.

Paul was elated to discover that there were eleven other Mensans attending the wedding: two Poles, three East Germans, five West Germans (who would, of course, all be German Mensans today) and another American. 'We all had a lot to learn about Polish weddings and wedding parties,' Paul observed.

The wedding ceremony was beautiful. It was held in a fifteenth-century Roman Catholic Church and the groom's brother sang part of the service. The church was unheated so there was absolutely no temptation for the guests to remove their overcoats and scarves in the below-freezing temperature.

The party began immediately following the church service. As soon as the food was brought to the tables in generous quantities Paul declared himself starving and began overindulging. He could not understand why he was the only one who appeared to be so hungry till it dawned on him that everyone else knew that there would be many, many more courses and had been pacing themselves accordingly. He had never seen such a wonderful assortment of foods and freely admitted that, although he did not always know what it was that he was eating, it was all delicious.

Dancing followed the meal and was a sight to behold. One dance involved each of the men placing an undisclosed sum of money in a hat on a chair for the honour of a dance with the bride. Other dances involved walking and acting 'ducklike' and yet another was the formation of an intertwining human chain.

If there is ever a vodka shortage in the world Paul will know why. Attendants were kept busy replacing empty vodka bottles with full ones. There were delicious local wines and, of course, that ubiquitous American contribution to *haute cuisine*, Coca-Cola.

The bride and groom are both professionals. Since the wedding Edward has completed his PhD in cybernetics at a Berlin university. Malgorzata is a practising oral surgeon. On the day after the wedding, when they were all having lunch together, Paul complained of stomach problems (not enough medicinal vodka, apparently). He had no sooner uttered the words than Malgorzata went to a nearby chemist, wrote a prescription on the spot and returned with the appropriate medicine.

The events on the day of his departure Paul described as unbelievable. His train was due to leave Wroclaw at 5 a.m. It was bitterly cold.

Malgorzata appeared at his hotel at 3.45 a.m., not only to drive him to the station but to accompany him on the eight-hour return journey to Warsaw. 'To say that I was overwhelmed by this gesture is an under-statement,' Paul said. 'This was the second day of her honeymoon.'

They arrived in Warsaw with several hours to spare before his flight. They toured the city and Paul had a glimpse of Lenin's statue, removed less than a month later (I should point out that its demise probably had nothing to do with Paul's visit). Shopping proved to be a sad task as state stores had very few goods to offer. In one there was a long queue of people hoping to buy toilet paper. A street vendor offered him a large lump of Baltic amber. At that point he had not learnt the value of amber and is still kicking himself for missing a bargain.

As his plane took off from Warsaw he realised that the world had become significantly smaller, thanks to Mensa.

Paul's visit to Oxford for the Ruby Anniversary was the beginning of a friendship with Goran Pettersson, then Mensa Sweden's Chairman. I have strongly contrasting memories of Goran. One is of him lying on the floor in Dallas urging his racing armadillo to the winning post by the time-honoured process of blowing hard on its nether regions, and the other is of his immaculate appearance at a formal dinner, resplen-dent in the dress uniform of a captain of the Swedish Army. It was, of course, quite easy for Paul and Goran to visit each other's country, though needless to say, our 'wanderkid' flew to Sweden by way of Iceland. 'One can hardly fly from the US to Stockholm without visiting Iceland,' Paul said.

There are few members in Reykjavik but he enjoyed meeting Bjorg Sigurvinsdottir, the more so because her son was the manager of the Reykjavik Hard Rock Café. He then joined Goran in his homes in Stockholm and Norrtalje. A boat trip to Helsinki took them to a Mensa Finland gathering where he renewed an old friendship with the Finnish Mensa Chairman, Osmo Renta.

Goran made a trip to South Carolina the following year and, following that, invited Paul to meet his wife-to-be in her native country, Scotland. Very shortly after their visit to Scotland an invitation arrived announcing the celebration in Norrtalje of Goran's 'peasant' wedding to the girl of his dreams.

In addition to the 'peasant' wedding there was to be a military wedding attended by fellow military officers from Sweden, Norway and Finland who would form a sword arch outside the church. Also invited was a mutual Mensa friend, Eugene Woznalk from South Carolina, a captain in the US Marine Corps. Eugene was asked to bring his Marine Corps dress-uniform and his sword so that he too could participate in the triumphal arch. The two of them were accompanied by a third guest, an expatriate South African, Niels Jensen.

A sword, even a ceremonial one, is regarded as a weapon by airline authorities and may not be taken on board an aeroplane as hand baggage. The matter was complicated by the fact that the sword was sensitive to cold and, in the unheated cargo hold of an aeroplane, could become brittle and break. Negotiations with cabin crew members got nowhere, but who better than two Mensans to persuade the flight captains to let the sword travel in the cockpit. All four arrived safely in Stockholm, one guest, one sword and two Mensans.

Many relations and friends of the bride-to-be, Francesca Ann, travelled from the UK to attend the wedding and, together with the others, managed to squeeze comfortably into the available quarters at Goran's Norrtalje home. The wedding preparations were in full swing; marquees were erected, flowers, food and drink were delivered and all was made ready for the great day.

In keeping with the customs of Swedish 'peasant' weddings the bride and groom drove to the church in a horse-drawn carriage, in this case a distance of about three kilometres, and, following tradition, were the last to arrive at the church. The service in the sixteenth-century church was short and uplifting. As the bride and groom emerged from the church the multinational military guard of honour formed their arch, under which the smiling couple walked.

The reception was held in a marquee. At the top table small flags indicated the nations of the attending guests, amongst them the present chairman of Swedish Mensa, a Hungarian, Jola Sigmund. The guests mingled and, after much eating, drinking and dancing, the wedding reception came to an end. The guests retired and the Americans prepared for their return flight early next day.

The Mensa world had become a little bit smaller once again. Should Paul ever tire of his job as management consultant specialising in labour relations, he would, I'm sure, make an excellent roving reporter of Mensa social events and relations.

PART TWO

CHAPTER 11

Mensa friendships

I t is stating the obvious to say that Mensa is about people, in this
instance people and their friendships. Over and over again I have
talked to members who claim that their lives have been enriched and
focused by the friends they have made in Mensa. Not everyone is lucky
enough to find common interests in their workplace, their homes or
even their social circle. Many are starved of good conversation; others,
frustrated by the lack of humour in those around them, become intro-
verted when the effort to communicate becomes more of a chore than a
pleasure.

'Have you ever started to say something and then stopped knowing
it would be a waste of time?' asked a lady from London Mensa (whom
I am calling Zoe). 'I have,' she continued, not waiting for an answer,
'and in the hope of finding some life out there before I really went gaga,

I took the Mensa test with a view to finding good and stimulating company.'

She needed no prompting to go on with her story. A divorced mother of three small children, she led a hectic life. Her days were taken up with her work and her evenings with household chores. Month followed month with no break in the dull routine. Her nerves were frayed; pills didn't help. Zoe loved her three youngsters but they were too young to be conversational companions. A breakdown was lurking in the background but she just could not afford the time to have it (my own is booked for April next). Desperate, she returned to her doctor's surgery, adding that she did not really hold out any hope of his being able to help, but at least, if nothing else, the little pink capsules dulled her mind. Her regular GP was on holiday and Zoe was annoyed that she had not been informed. As she made another appointment his locum appeared at her elbow. The motherly-looking lady asked if she could be of help and Zoe, not wanting to consult a stranger but too embarrassed to leave, followed her into the familiar consulting room. She asked for a repeat prescription for the faintly soothing, if ineffective tablets. The kindly stranger read her medical file and then asked her why she felt the need to take them. Zoe felt fury sweep over her in a wave and then recede. Being a very self-contained person she was astonished to hear her own voice blurting out all her frustrations and worries. No interruption came from the patient listener. Zoe sat back totally drained. 'This may or may not help you, but it is worth a try,' said the smiling doctor. 'When you get home just check to see if you have had this prescription in the past.' Thanking her and feeling slightly better at having got a lot off her chest, Zoe went home. 'How can I remember what I have taken in the past?' she asked herself. She fished the prescription out of her pocket; it contained two words, 'Contact Mensa'. Zoe was furious. What on earth had that to do with her problems? She had not taken time off from work for this nonsense.

Later that evening, when calmer, she thought of the offending piece of paper. Her annoyance turned to flattery; the doctor must have thought she was intelligent or she would not have suggested contacting Mensa. Was the doctor a member? Maybe it would be worth while following up the suggestion. If nothing else, she reasoned, it would be interesting to know her IQ. Zoe laughed for the first time in ages when she thought what an idiot she would have looked had she handed that prescription to a pharmacist.

She applied for the home test; the result was promising. This encouraged her to sit the supervised test. Even better, she qualified to join. A neighbour, one of her few friends, shared her good news and, despite her own busy life, offered to care for the children for her whilst she attended her first meeting.

In a buoyant mood, but with a slight fluttering of the heart, she made her way to the venue, a local pub. Four or five people sitting in a group looked like what she considered to be 'the type', but they turned out to be business people having a late and liquid meeting. As she murmured her apologies, wondering why she had typecast Mensans as boozy businessmen, someone touched her arm, introduced himself and led her to a table in an alcove. 'Great start,' she thought. She found herself in an eclectic bunch of men, women and youths dressed in anything from formal city wear to torn jeans. At first she was shy and spoke only when more or less dragged into the conversation. Gradually, though, her reserve faded and by the end of the evening, aided by a little Dutch courage, she was putting in her two penn'orth with the best of them.

Zoe returned home elated. The evening had been stimulating and the next one could not come soon enough. It was an eating meeting and was as challenging and even more enjoyable than the first one. Life took on a rosier glow and Zoe kicked herself for not having thought of joining sooner.

Three months went by and then she heard the awful news, her kind friend and neighbour was moving to another town. No neighbour, no babysitter and, worst of all, no Mensa meetings. Zoe telephoned to cancel her booking for the next eating meeting, thinking miserably that she would probably never attend anything again.

Her lifeline had been severed. She mooched about the house on the night of the meeting. Self-pity ruled once more.

A couple of days later the telephone rang. 'We missed you at the meeting and hear you have a sitter problem,' burbled a chirpy voice. For a moment Zoe could not put a name to it, then the clogged cogs of her mind began to click and she knew who her caller was. 'I'm phoning to offer my niece's services as a babysitter. You need have no fear, she's a very responsible girl.'

Two of our Mensa friendships began when a letter from Florida arrived at the Irish Mensa office. It is to the memory of one of these friends, Bob Gordon, that I dedicate this chapter.

An American Mensan, Lee Cooper, wrote to say that he would be in Dublin for the Irish Mensa Annual Gathering and would be happy to give a talk on hypnotherapy during the weekend. David wrote back accepting his offer gladly and, by way of a personal note, told him that we hoped to be in his area within the next couple of months.

We were celebrating our silver wedding with the holiday of a lifetime – a Caribbean cruise. David, knowing how much I disliked flying, had arranged this trip as a wonderful surprise. (When he reads this he will learn that I was equally nervous at the thought of crossing the Atlantic in the middle of March on a ship which had, in my mind, diminished to the size of a rowing boat.) A further letter from Lee confirmed he would pay us a visit when the ship docked in Fort Lauderdale, Florida.

With the good wishes of family and friends we set out, leaving strict instructions that they should not contact us unless a dire emergency arose. The vast ocean was as calm as a mill pond. My worries proved to be groundless. There was something to do every minute of the day and night, we met terrific people and everything on the sea was rosy until, one afternoon, we heard our name being called to take a ship-to-shore telephone call. It was at that moment that we experienced the inability to walk. We knew that unless it was something very serious we would not be contacted in mid-Atlantic. Finally, as if walking through quicksand and with out hearts pumping lumpy custard, we reached the radio cabin where David, his face chalky white, picked up the receiver. It was not a dreaded announcement from home – it was Lee Cooper. Relief was a mild way of expressing our feelings at that moment. He had discovered from the shipping line that, due to security, no visitors were to be permitted on board and he suggested that we meet him at the quay-side.

In our after-panic we had forgotten to ask him how we would recognise him. When we arrived at port a couple of days later and about three hours behind schedule we played it by ear. Surrounded by hundreds of embarking and disembarking (and many just barking) passengers, we had no hesitation in approaching Lee Cooper. Clad in a straw boater, complete with fresh carnation sticking straight up from the brim, and carrying a small, folding table, a bottle of champagne, several plastic cups and an ice box, stood a figure we knew had to be a Mensan. Presenting me with the flower, he introduced himself and another Mensa member, Bob Gordon, who had accompanied him for what he described later as 'the hell of it'.

As we sat drinking and talking in the busy embarkation area, almost impervious to the startled and amused glances of passers-by, we recounted the reason for our late arrival in Florida.

That morning, anchored off the coast of Florida, we were perfectly positioned to watch the Space Shuttle blast off for the first time into the clear blue sky. By six o'clock in the morning everyone on board was crowded on deck to witness the historic event. Fruit juices, tea and coffee were served as we waited in the chilly air, and the arrival of helicopters bearing camera crews and reporters added to the excitement. There was a direct radio link to Cape Kennedy and we were able to follow the preparations for the flight – history in the making. The craft was clearly visible to the naked eye and the excited passengers on the decks fell silent as the countdown began. Suddenly a call to abort reached our ears and the counting stopped. One of the computers had malfunctioned and, hoping that this would merely cause a delay, we continued our wait. It proved to be in vain, for after another hour of patient watching and listening the captain reluctantly announced that it would be impossible to remain any longer. The camera crews and reporters returned to their waiting helicopters and the disappointed passengers slowly headed to the dining room for breakfast as the anchors were raised and we headed south. A really disappointing end to what should have been such an exciting event.

As we told the tale Lee Cooper nodded knowingly. The reason for his wry smile proved to be his full understanding and knowledge of the situation. He had recently taken early retirement from the position of rocket-testing engineer at Cape Kennedy and knew only too well the problems and difficulties of launching rockets into space. We listened fascinated as he filled us in on the vagaries of rocketry and space travel.

Having retired at a very early age, he enrolled in the University of Florida and, purely as a hobby, had taken a course in hypnotherapy which he practised for anyone in need of support, particularly in respect of surgical procedures.

During this time Bob Gordon had said very little. He was a tall, well-built man with twinkling eyes and a ready smile. He had met Lee for the first time the previous night at a Mensa party which Bob had hosted at his home. Lee had mentioned he was going to meet us and invited Bob to come along.

All too soon the warning bellow of the siren sounded. As we prepared to leave, David and Lee made their arrangements for Lee's trip to Dublin. We said goodbye to Bob and hoped we would have an opportunity to meet again; he quietly admitted he would be joining the ship on its return call at Fort Lauderdale and then journeying to England – he would contact us.

The Caribbean was not as kind as the Atlantic and the ship pitched and tossed angrily. It was fun to watch dancing passengers start at one end of the floor and, with the sway of the ship, slide effortlessly to the other.

A couple of the ports were too small for the ship to berth, so it anchored off shore and passengers were ferried to land in launches. One such stop had more than its fair share of buffeting as the small boat banged against the side of the ship jarring and jolting its occupants. There were very few passengers on that short journey who were sorry to arrive on dry land. We explored the tiny Island of St Martin, but David suggested we return to the ship; he was suffering from back problems and it did not take too long to see he was in trouble. We made our return journey to Florida with David confined to bed. Very soon after the ship sailed from Fort Lauderdale, Bob telephoned our room. David explained his predicament and apologised, and Bob offered to come to the cabin to visit us for a few minutes. Two hours later he left and so began a much cherished friendship.

He returned after dinner and I left the two of them talking and went to join some friends for a drink. As I turned into the corridor a little later, I was greeted by roars of laughter coming through the open cabin door. Despite the air conditioning the cabin was very hot, adding to

David's discomfort. As he said good night Bob remarked that he hadn't laughed so much for years, and his visit had certainly done David a lot of good. He was a marvellous companion for the three remaining days of our return journey to New York, and his cheerful manner and fund of stories turned a very miserable episode into a much happier one.

Naturally in the time we spent together, both then and in later years, we swopped stories of events in our lives and, his proved to have been most interesting.

He had worked hard as a young man to put himself through college. He had taken a year off to earn the money to pay for further tuition but it was a hard struggle as his parents were divorced and he had to support his mother as well as himself. He graduated from Harvard. As it was then war time he joined the army and was posted to Adak, in the Aleutian Islands, with the responsibility of operating a radio station. Life was not too hectic and he had plenty of time to write an article for the Saturday Evening Post which, when accepted for publication, earned him enough money to propose to and subsequently marry his girl friend.

Married life for them began in army quarters. They had very little money and, when the war ended, they moved to Canada where he became an importer of cutlery from Sheffield.

Several years later and, no doubt having proved his ability, his father in law invited Bob to join him in his successful real estate and property development business. They moved to Florida and he was involved in the buying and selling of land. They started the city of Miramar, which today is a well populated and thriving city. All the land they bought was swamp. His description of how the land was turned into stable ground suitable for building made fascinating listening. The dredging of this marshy land was a monumental task but, eventually, with lines drawn and channels to carry the water, it began to take shape.

One day, shortly after the work had been started, they were contacted by another developer who was anxious to purchase their land. Deciding it would do no harm to hear what the man had to say they agreed to a meeting. Bob and his father-in-law did their homework as to the value and, accompanied by their lawyer, made their way to the appointed meeting place. The developer and his lawyer arrived on time. Pleasantries were exchanged and the prospective purchasers informed them that they would make only one offer and that it would not be open to discussion, take it or leave it. This was agreed by all parties and the amount was written on a piece of paper, folded in half and passed across the table. Bob unfolded the paper, looked at it and said that he wished to discuss the matter with his father-in-law and their lawyer. The three of them left the room. He said that they looked at each other with incredulous disbelief. The offer was almost five times their decided asking price! Was there a hidden gold mine that they did not know about? Buried pirate treasure? Liberace's suits or Elvis's underwear? Playing it very cool they returned to the meeting room and reluctantly accepted the offer – with the exception of a small, unimportant section which they wished to retain for themselves – and the deal was struck and the contract signed. It was on the retained section of this swamp land that Bob later built his lovely home.

Giving up the real estate business after some time he entered the banking world and remained there until his retirement.

As the years passed, Bob, his wife and their three children often visited Europe. They fell in love with London, its theatres, museums, shopping, the culture and the people. Now widowed, he still tried to visit his favourite city annually. Before we left the ship at New York we persuaded him to come to Dublin for the Annual Gathering, assuring him that it was only a short hop from his adopted city of London.

The Gathering took place about three weeks after our return and we were happy that, true to their promises, both Lee and Bob arrived in Dublin for the long weekend. The Irish Mensa Committee did their usual good job of organising and, more importantly, welcoming members and visitors alike. Over the years the reputation for friendliness and warmth has spread and the Irish Mensa Annual Gathering has found a special place in the diaries of its many visitors.

Lee gave his talk and demonstration on hypnotherapy. Starting with an explanation of how it worked he assured people that it was really a form of self-hypnosis and nothing to be feared. Its many benefits included the treatment of phobias and some addictions, and it promoted relaxation. It was particularly interesting for me to learn that holidays and travelling were, for some people, very traumatic and, for nervous flyers and sailors, not the happy experiences they should have been. Had he known me better at the time I would have thought that this information was for my benefit! He then asked everyone present to close their eyes and relax. Speaking softly, he suggested that we should imagine ourselves in a peaceful garden on a warm, sunny day, water running gently from a small stream, birds singing and bees humming. With our recent summers it really did need a vivid imagination. Instructing people to open their eyes again, he enquired how long we thought that section had taken. My guess was about five minutes; I was amazed to learn that it was twelve.

The following day there was a mystery tour. David announced that this was a mystery tour with a difference – the passengers knew where they were going but no one would tell the driver. He skilfully dodged the missiles aimed at his head.

Our two American friends thoroughly enjoyed the weekend and Bob returned to London promising to keep in touch. Lee spent another couple of days in Dublin in order to see more of the city. We had dinner together and he gave us a vivid description of his early days, growing up in New York.

His family moved to Miami in Florida with the intention of opening a restaurant. Their research took them to many local eateries as they watched carefully and noted everything in order to avoid mistakes and collect ideas. One evening on their usual quest they went to one busy restaurant. In those days there was no air-conditioning he explained, so it was customary to wear a short sleeved white shirt and dark slacks. Seated at a table and waiting for service, Lee, his father and their partner noticed the extremely harassed owner attempting to appease waiting customers. Enquiring as to the problem, he told them that most of the staff had failed to turn up and that it was very difficult for him to manage on his own. Leaving their table the three of them, dressed in similar fashion to a waiter, quickly donned aprons and started to serve the impatient diners. They finally opened their own establishment and it became famous. 'Famous' was its name as well as its reputation.

Apart from being a rocket testing engineer, a hypnotherapist, restaurateur, concessionaire, lecturer, cosmetics distributor, riding master at a dude ranch, photographer and a hotelier, Lee's contention was that this proved that either Mensans can do anything they put their minds to ... or, cannot keep a job! He is still undecided.

He entered the City College of New York at the tender age of fifteen. At eighteen he served in the Army until the war ended. He then helped his father to establish the restaurant and returned to his alma mater where he graduated with a Bachelor of Mechanical Engineering degree. He then worked for Bell Aircraft in the days, he said, when nobody really knew what they were doing.

'We would improvise a test stand, put a rudimentary engine on it and blow it up, then try to work out why it went wrong. It's a wonder any of us came out alive,' he laughed. He returned to Florida and joined his father in opening and running a three hundred seat restaurant in Miami. It was during this time that he took his flying lessons and, one day, was almost arrested when he, with his instructor, tried to land on the highly restricted strip of Cape Canaveral (the missile test site) thinking it was Melbourne City airport. (They were still in the US, MC Airport was quite close to Canaveral). Not content with tempting fate in this instance they tried for the double by flying over an anti-aircraft artillery practice firing range. By now he was beginning to wonder about this instructor!

Possibly his brief airborne look at Cape Canaveral prompted his return to the world of rocket testing. In those days there were long delays during countdowns in order to repair problems which cropped up so frequently. During one such delay the manager of a sub-contractor got bored and took off with one of the secretaries to a wooded area, near the beach but still within the Cape grounds, for a romantic interlude. Their luck had deserted them when they were caught *in flagrante delicto* by a roving security patrol. At a loss as to what charge should be brought against the errant Romeo and Juliet they came up with 'being in a secure area without wearing their identification badges!' Lee then went to Denver in Colarado to set up test procedures for the new Titan Missile and then on to the Space Technology Labs in Los Angeles where they supervised all missile and Space programmes for the Air Force.

For no apparent reason he then switched professions again and built and ran a motel in Orlando, Florida. No contractor, no knowledge of construction and no experience. It worked. Back to engineering with the Aerospace Corporation for five years. This was followed by something completely different. Cosmetic production and distribution.

By this time we were dizzy with the diversity of it all but, there was more. He completed and ran a family-owned hotel in Sarasota and then he built, operated and still owns a hotel in Key West, on the Florida Keys.

Not content with this full time occupation it was then that he enrolled in Miami University to take his degree in Hypnosis, earning his right to practice.

Being a lover of travel Lee has attended Mensa gatherings all over the world and his wandering life has, to date, taken him to thirty seven countries on six continents.

His time in Dublin was ended. The weekends or even weeks which we were subsequently to spend together never seemed to be long enough.

Two years passed and we kept in touch with cards and an occasional letter (most Mensans, I have discovered, do not like writing letters). Our next meeting was the result of a pessimistic attitude. Let me explain. I came home from the local garage one day with a fist full of competition leaflets, each of which had a bubble caption to be completed – the prize was a holiday for two. David raised a sceptical eyebrow. 'A waste of time,' he declared. 'It isn't,' I insisted. 'If you're not in, you can't win.'

Being of a kindly nature, he allowed himself to be press-ganged into composing the appropriate humorous captions. He did, however, take a stand by refusing to write our name and address on any of them; that he left to me. Many weeks passed and I forgot all about the competition, until a letter arrived congratulating us – we had won a holiday of our choice for two.

I am a creature of impulse and I found it very difficult not to telephone David immediately to tell him the exciting news, but I did manage to contain myself. After dinner that evening I casually mentioned the competition and asked if he thought the results would be announced shortly. 'You really are an incurable optimist,' he said patiently but pityingly. Unable to wait a moment longer, I passed him the envelope. He did not blush – but it was a reasonable imitation.

We contacted Bob and Lee. Bob invited us to stay with him and was gratefully but firmly refused. At this stage we felt it would be an imposition to land on his doorstep, but we did arrange to stay at a hotel near his home in Hollywood, Florida.

Bob collected us at the airport and took us to his home. Unlike its glittering Californian namesake, this was a quiet residential town, boasting none of the tourist attractions of other nearby resorts. Bob's bungalow was at the end of a quiet street and, to our delight, had a swimming pool which led almost immediately on to one of the many narrow waterways which threaded their way to the sea.

A miserable, cold summer had left us starved of sunshine and we were delighted with the warm, sunny Florida weather. Lazing by the hotel swimming pool one morning, we saw two waiters carrying champagne approach a large cluster of people sitting at a couple of tables near us. We were just starting to play our usual game of solving a mystery without knowing a single relevant fact, when our attention was diverted by a small, low-flying aeroplane. As we watched, the pilot began to sky-write and, little by little, a message began to appear.

'Will you marry me?' we read in the cloudless sky. When the proposal was completed and the smoke switched off, a girl who had been sitting amongst the people at the champagne-filled tables was instructed to turn round. She was open-mouthed, and all around her people were on their feet clapping. One lady, unable to bear the suspense (it was not me, honestly) shouted, 'Well, will you?'

The pretty girl was totally gobsmacked. Had she had any thoughts of refusing the proposal, the interest and encouragement of all the eager onlookers would have made it impossible for her to do so. Shyly she nodded. Her boyfriend (who had just become her fiancé) beamed, his mother cried (we decided she was his mother because she was clinging to his arm), and everyone in the party drank their champagne as the poolsiders returned to normality.

A Mensa New Year's Eve party at Bob's was a fun night. We were pleased to meet Floridian Mensans and also many of his personal friends, the most familiar of whom was Lee Cooper. We found it quite unreal celebrating the turn of the year in a tropical garden beneath a star-filled sky. Midnight was heralded by the hooters of hundreds of small boats in the vicinity, and all was well with the world.

New Year's Day was a long week. Bob called for us early in the morning. All signs of the previous night's party had vanished; enormous containers of popcorn were standing on tables placed in front of the tele-

vision, and we had become invisible. People arrived, and when introduced gave us a cursory greeting without any of the friendliness to which
we had become accustomed. The reason? The Florida Orange Bowl –
American football on the large TV screen. The game was not too easy
to follow; everyone present was totally engrossed and could only explain
the rules spasmodically between cries of derision, disappointment or
encouragement. The popcorn vanished, people helped themselves to
drinks and food, David snoozed.

The day, however, was not totally wasted. A lady I had met the previous evening, who turned out to be as uninitiated in the game as I was,
noticed that I had removed an earring which was hurting me. She told
me to stick the rod of the earring into a clove of garlic and then replace
it in my ear. This had to be done three times a day for three days at a
time when my ear was not sore. I thanked her, but thought to myself
that this sounded like an old wives' tale. Ever since I had my ears pierced
at the age of seventeen (a couple of years ago), they had acted up every
couple of months, often becoming really uncomfortable. When I
returned home I remembered the lady's advice and thought, 'I have nothing to lose, I'll try it.' It worked. I was ashamed of my scepticism as from
that day on the problem has never recurred. Vampires have not both-
ered me either.

The evening finished around midnight and, with great fortitude
and selfless courage, we have resisted the temptation ever to watch
American football again. Bob, by way of apology, offered to watch a
cricket match so that we could have our revenge. We agreed but decided
to wait before telling him that we found cricket equally boring. The
laugh, however, was on us when he confessed later that he loved to
watch cricket even though he could not make head nor tail of its rules.

Lee came to visit us at the hotel accompanied by a friend whom we
had met at the New Year's Eve party. Little did we know then that this
lady, Margie, was destined to become his wife. It was on this evening that
I learned to speak English with a Brooklyn accent. This was the lesson
verbatim. 'Toity doity poiple boids sittin' on de koib, choipin' an' boipin'
an' eatin' doity woims!' There's just no end to my linguistic ability.

One morning Bob telephoned to say we had been invited to a Mensa
party that evening. He called for us earlier than usual saying he wanted

to show us something, but would not tell us what. When he turned the car into a small cul-de-sac (no, he was not a magician), we were unprepared for the sight that met our eyes: a bungalow half way along the road was festooned from roof to road (or sidewalk if you prefer), with every conceivable form of Christmas decoration. On the roof, in an effect caused by hundreds of flickering coloured lights, Santa Claus moved backwards and forwards in his sleigh, pulled by at least eight reindeer. The bungalow itself, with all its windows and doors outlined by a solid ribbon of light, was probably visible from Mars. A large, brightly lit nativity scene stood in the garden. The three wise men, bearing their gifts, were highlighted by powerful arc lamps hidden behind large mounds of brightly wrapped gifts. Lights covered every branch of every bush and tree. Stars shone and twinkled, elves worked at wrapping gifts and more reindeer waited patiently, their antlers blinking on and off, while their noses were stopping traffic half way to Oralndo.

We were not the only visitors viewing the amazing sight; the narrow road was full of cars for its fame had spread. The thousands of watts made it almost as bright as day and showed up the muddy tracks and flattened grass of the surrounding gardens. Bob assured us that there were no problems with the neighbours as the owner of this festive delight, the director of a funeral home, supplied cases of wine to sooth furrowed brows until the damage repaired itself. David, ever the romantic, was, I assumed, admiring the amazing enterprise. I learned later that he was only trying to calculate the wattage and giving fervent thanks that the electricity bill would not be landing on his doormat.

When we reached our original destination, the Mensa party, we were met at the gates of the house and the car was whisked away. This was the first and only time we have encountered valet parking at a Mensa gathering. The host was standing for election to the city council and celebrating his birthday as well. The house was packed to the rafters. Bob was like the Pied Piper, everyone who knew him came to say hello and we met many of his followers. By this time we were beginning to take the balmy nights for granted and, as we wandered outside to the pool area, we discovered that the house was only a few feet from the Atlantic Ocean. The lights of the town and the sea-going craft were reflected in the still water. People wandered in the garden or sat in groups by the pool. We talked to one lady who proved to be the artist of the owl, Mensa's unofficial symbol, which has since appeared in many of the Society's publications.

The two weeks vanished in a flash. Bob promised to visit us the following summer when he made his annual pilgrimage to his adopted city. Lee took a rain check not knowing his future plans.

Infrequent letters were exchanged, the date for Bob's visit was fixed and we made our plans for his visit. June was rainin' out all over. Not a single rose was in bloom – so embarrassing as we had promised Bob every bush would be laden with the perfumed flowers that grew so beautifully in our temperate climate, and which he struggled to grow under the tropical sun.

Bob telephoned from London to say he had been joined by a friend from the US. We assured him she would be welcome, so she came to Dublin with him. We made plans to show them around the city, to take them out for dinner and, on the Saturday of their visit, friends invited us for drinks and to a buffet and, in turn, we invited several of our friends to a brunch to meet them.

Everything was organised (miracles do happen!). The morning of the brunch I awoke about seven o'clock. The house was quiet as I tiptoed downstairs to put the food on the table, which had been extended from a round one to an oblong by the addition of two leaves. Happily drinking a cup of tea as I placed the platters and bowls on the table it was soon ready and, standing back to view the finished effect, to my horror and in slow motion I watched the centre of the table slowly folding with the bowls and plates converging towards their inevitable destination – the floor. 'Don't panic,' I told myself as I panicked. Somehow, with my arms stretched to their limit and beyond I reached the sides of the table and managed to prevent them parting totally. The offending leaves clicked back into place and, with my heart in my mouth, I let go of one of the sides in order to lock it. It held and the calamitous 'foodslide' was averted. The leaves are now clearly marked one to four in indelible ink.

As Bob had never seen anything of Ireland except Dublin, we had arranged to take them for a night to Marlfield House, a lovely country hotel in Wexford. We left early in the morning and, finally, the June sun popped its head out from behind the clouds. Bob was entranced by the scenery: the young lambs gambolled in the fields, the purple mountains stretched for miles as a back-drop and, as we reached Wicklow, the sea, with its roller-coasting waves, added to the charm of the beautiful countryside.

We enjoyed our short stay in Wexford, touring the area and showing them as much as we could in the short time allotted. As always, in Bob's company, we found that time ran out too quickly. We had to speed to the airport, but even this hair-raising journey failed to disturb his good humour – though he did look a little pale.

The next time the Three Musketeers, Bob, Lee and David, were together was the following summer at Mensa at Cambridge. Lynda (our daughter) was by this time living in London; she travelled to Cambridge with David and, after surviving unmerciful teasing and the sharp wit of Bob and Lee, gave her unstinting stamp of approval to the friendship. Bob's daughter flew over to spend some time with him in London and Bob contacted Lynda and took his two 'daughters' out for lunch. Both of our children were as fond of him as we were.

Another two years went by; we received repeated invitations and Bob threatened to make no more Irish visits unless we returned to Florida. This time we accepted graciously. Not one word did I utter about my reservations of going to Florida in September, the hurricane season. We were routed through New York, and there we took our seats on an over-booked plane. The ticket director offered all sorts of inducements to get people to travel on a later flight, but my seat belt was fastened and was going to remain so. When the mess of irate passengers had been sorted out, we took off for Florida. 'Ladies and gentlemen, welcome on board.' The pilot sounded laid back. 'We are making a slight detour today to avoid Hurricane ...'

I never did hear its name. Why had they not informed us before we took off? Why had they not given us the option of staying on terra firma, instead of letting us risk our lives at the mercy of this vicious phenomenon? If people were meant to fly, I reasoned, they would have been born with a passport. My mental ranting was interrupted by a stewardess offering drinks. The plane was steady as a rock as I sipped what I was sure was my last drink in this life.

'Hey, wow! Look at that,' said a passenger. Slowly but surely everyone on the left hand side crossed over to the right, leaving me alone to balance the plane. (Well, someone had to, didn't they?) 'You must see this,' said David, 'it's incredible.' Reluctantly I allowed him to unweld my seat belt and, half standing, I peered across the aisle and through the window. Not a ripple disturbed us as cautiously I eased myself out of my seat. He was not exaggerating; it was a stunning sight. The sky was an azure blue, the sun was shining brightly, but, looking downwards, I saw the blue turning to yellow and then to grey and, finally, to an incredible jet black. Enormous flashes of lightning lit the comparatively small section of ebony sky and streaked towards the ground. The awesome hurricane passed quickly from our vision as the plane hurtled towards our destination.

Bob's smiling face was a welcome sight at the airport and he wasted no time in whisking us through the evening traffic to the quiet, peaceful bungalow. The following day, as we were sitting in the garden, we heard a car horn honk and a door slam – Lee Cooper had arrived. This time he was carrying a large tub of Häagen Dazs ice cream and a navy-blue box. A delightful feeling of *déjà vu* – the old team was back in action.

Barely taking time to dump the frosted container, Lee called us to a table and took the lid off the intriguing box. This, he enthused, was the very latest game and was really fascinating. We settled ourselves around the table and examined the contents – a game board, hundreds of cards and some coloured markers. In short, Trivial Pursuit. Pausing only long enough to eat, we played for hours. As dusk fell we moved inside and continued the competitive game, which was by then reaching a crucial stage. I was all set to claim victory; silence fell as Lee read my question: 'What is the prefix for the Chicago telephone exchange?'

'Not fair,' I claimed.

'Yes it is,' answered David.

'Not really,' said the soft-hearted Bob.

'The luck of the draw,' ventured Lee, half-heartedly.

'Rotten lot.' I sulked and resisted the temptation to flick the ice cream on my spoon at the offending card. Fair play triumphed and the gentlemanly decision was reached – the question should be replaced. My luck ran out this time as I didn't know the answer; I had lost my golden opportunity to beat the male Mensa brains.

The weather was hot and humid. We sat at the pool. Bob taught us how to tackle the crosswords in the *New York Times* and the *Wall Street Journal*. We agonised over a puzzle of Scrabble words with spellings strange to our eyes. We played Trivial Pursuit, solved the world's problems, mentally invented savoury ice creams, played Trivial Pursuit, learned of the danger to the ozone layer and played Trivial Pursuit. We gave new Latin names to trees and shrubs, went out for dinner, came home and – that's right – played Trivial Pursuit.

Lee joined us at the weekend and they took us to a jai a-lai game. They explained the rules and the betting procedures scientifically; for some unknown reason I ignored their advice and put my cents on the numbers I fancied. The Male Mensa Team (for that is what they had become) all lost; I won. They made me buy the ice cream – they insisted. Home we went and settled down to play ... Wrong! – Scrabble. This was a very serious game, even more serious than – you know what. No leniency was shown towards suspect words. Lee, the essence of kindness and generosity, became very strict when faced with a game board.

The weather became even hotter and the humidity rose to equal the temperature. The television weather forecasters were tracking hurricanes which originated in Africa. Bob's mother came to visit him, a marvellously humorous and feisty lady approaching her ninetieth birthday. She told us she was hanging around 'to make damn sure I get that telegram from the President'.

At this stage Hurricane Isadore was picking up momentum and heading for the Florida coast. The television gave half-hourly updates and Bob reassured us there was no cause for alarm. Storm shutters, with narrow perspex peepholes, could be bolted to the ground around the bungalow and everything was well protected. The warnings escalated hourly. Considerable damage had already been caused in the Caribbean islands as the hurricane approached the mainland. At midnight Bob decided it was time to take action; we went outside and began to put the shutters in place. Even this was fun. We pushed tables and chairs inside the tracks; everything that could be moved was safely stored before the sturdy metal sheets formed their cocoon. The air was still and silent and, almost unbelievably, the temperature rose even higher. The silence was eerie.

Next morning we awoke to silence. We were still in one piece and, switching on the television, we discovered that just as it hit the tip of the coastline the hurricane had suddenly veered out to sea. The damage had been minimal.

Lee telephoned the next day to say he had to go to the Florida Keys on business and asked if we would all care to join him? David and I were delighted; this was somewhere we had always wanted to visit. We set off in Bob's car, crossing over the Seven Mile Bridge.

Lee gave us a conducted tour of the area, promising to take us to see the sunset for which Key West is famous. We left our hotel half an hour before the scheduled time of the sunset and strolled to the viewing spot. this was a meeting point for everyone on Key West: roller-skating jugglers, a piper in full regalia, a mime artist and singers all entertained the onlookers. Colourfully dressed youngsters made punks, with their garish hair and odd dress, look staid as they paraded up and down seeking admiration. The atmosphere was lively, friendly and expectant as the world and his wife waited for the big moment.

The spectacular disappearance of the sun into the sea was always applauded. That evening the sunset was awarded seven out of ten by its regular coterie of aficionados. We then ate in a lovely little restaurant in the town and were shown the bar where Ernest Hemingway is rumoured to have spent a considerable amount of his time. Trivial Pursuit had, of course, travelled with us, and the ongoing game was – ongoing.

The following morning we took a tram tour to see the whole of Key West plus its mountain. The mountain is about eight feet high – the locals are very proud of it but, back home, we have taller potholes!

After lunch we took the Scrabble down to the little man-made beach. David read his book and the three of us played. Scores were very much level and the board was well covered as we reached the end of the letters. A triple word score was open, Bob was frowning, Lee was smiling. I saw a way to block it and still leave myself with a blank tile and an 'S'. (For non Scrabble players these are useful and valuable score makers). Placing two of my remaining tiles in order to block the triple word, Lee challenged. Lee was correct – the word 'rhea' was misspelt. I had left the 'H' out.

Disappointed that my bluff had been called and, assuming from Lee's grin that he could place all his letters and that, yet again, I would be pipped at the post, I leaned over to have a look at Bob's remaining tiles. He had a 'Q' and an 'X'. They were unplaceable at this stage of the game. The scores were level. David, having finished his reading, asked Lee a question and, nudging Non, I swopped my two valuable tiles for his useless ones. We were both laughing hysterically as Bob placed them on the board with a flourish. Poor Lee. He could not believe his eyes. He had been waiting to use his remaining letters and claim the game. Well Lee, I humbly apologise and, although it was irresistible at the time, it has been on my conscience ever since.

With only a couple of days left we returned to Hollywood; the remaining time vanished in what seemed like a minute. Bob promised to visit us the following summer. Again Lee was unsure of his plans.

Some months later we learned that Lee had undergone triple by-pass surgery. He was well on the road to recovery and his hypnotherapy had helped him enormously. He had paid several visits to the surgeon prior to the operation and had been talked through the procedure step by step. Lee prepared himself by self-hypnosis. After the operation, the surgeon informed him that, as a result of his ability to reduce his own heart rate and bleeding, even though heavily anaesthetised, this had been the easiest triple by-pass operation he had ever performed and that it had taken an hour less than usual.

Early in June, Bob telephoned from London. Because of terrorist threats to US airlines, Americans were staying away in droves. He had planned to bring a couple of his older grandchildren with him but, fearful of the problems, their parents had reluctantly cancelled the trip, leaving Bob with a two-bedroomed apartment. Would we go and stay with him, he asked? Quite by chance, David had to be in London the following weekend for a meeting, so we were delighted with the unexpected bonus. We as always took up where we had left off – this time minus Trivial Pursuit.

The time passed pleasantly; we browsed in the antique markets, visited the shops and lounged around the flat reading the papers. Bob took us to a tiny French restaurant which specialised in light-as-air cheese soufflés. We decided to walk back to the apartment after the meal, but the London Marathon was in progress, making it impossible to go anywhere. We went to a pavement café and sat watching the breathless contestants pass by. The only person we recognised in that seething mass of runners was Lorraine Boyce, British Mensa's Local Secretaries' Officer.

We asked Bob what he would like to do when he came to Dublin the following week. 'I just like to be with you and David,' he said. 'Would you like us to invite a few friends for a drink?' I asked. My offer was politely refused.

We offered to take Bob for a drive the morning after his arrival; he said he would prefer to sit and chat. This was no problem as we never had any shortage of things to talk about. He filled me in on his life, his problems and his romantic entanglements. We went out for dinner. We were all totally comfortable in one another's company. He wanted us to spend Christmas with him; David said we would think about it. We promised to let him know as we said our familiar goodbyes.

One month later we received a distressed telephone call from a lovely friend of his (and ours), Isabel, who informed us Bob was in hospital recovering from a heart attack. We were, needless to say, very upset and telephoned him immediately. We were happy to hear his chirpy voice; with his usual lack of complaint he made light of the attack and repeated that he was looking forward to seeing us at Christmas. Not wanted to upset him, David agreed we would go. We realised that Bob must have been ill on his last visit. This explained his lack of enthusiasm for outings he would normally have enjoyed. Typically, he had said nothing.

Three weeks later Isabel telephoned again. When we heard her weeping, unable to speak, we were left in no doubt as to what had happened.

Bob was an irreplaceable friend, and we remember him as a happy, funny, caring, generous, gentle, gentleman. We shall never forget him. It was all due to Mensa that we got to know Bob and Lee. We look forward to our next meeting with Lee, now happily married to Margie, whom he met at a Regional Gathering in Atlanta. We value his friendship as highly as we did Bob's.

All too often people ask, 'But what does Mensa actually do?' Mensa does not 'do' anything. Its aims are to find and foster intelligence and to serve its members. The members take from and put into Mensa what they want to, but I am sure that for a huge number of Mensans the friendships they make are the most valued part of their membership.

An article sent to me by American Mensan, E. Jimmee Stein, attests to this. She has had to tackle the same question in a different form. 'Why should Mensa have a cause?' Her response to this: during her 'grand tour' of Europe, which began in London, she used the Mensa International Register to contact a former resident of the United States, Milton Subotsky, who was currently living in London. He collected her from her hotel and took her out to lunch. He then took her to a railway station, bought her a ticket, put her on a train and instructed her to get off at Blackheath. She was somewhat frightened and begged for an explanation, but her pleas fell on deaf ears. Milton kissed her on the cheek and all he would say was, 'Get off at Blackheath.'

When she got out of the train she found herself alone on the platform. The figure of a man emerged from the darkness. Suddenly everything became clear. E. Jimmee recognised the man from photographs; it was Victor Serebriakoff. She was not sure which was the greater, the shock of meeting the Honorary Secretary of Mensa (as he was then) or the relief that she was no longer alone at that deserted station. She spent a lovely evening with Victor and his charming wife Win.

Other names in the Mensa Register came to life for E. Jimmee in London, Edinburgh and Paris. 'Every Mensa member I met was warm, cordial and delightful to be with. Our common "cause" was that we were all members of Mensa. That was all we needed,' she said.

Continuing her story, she told of receiving the sad news of her father's passing. This came from her father's attorney in Los Angeles and left her and her brother Larry in deep sorrow. Several days later came another call from Los Angeles informing them that their father's attorney had died of a heart attack.

Brother and sister were left not only grieving but bewildered; their father's estate involved children of two marriages. In desperation E. Jimmee turned to the Mensa Office for help. Margot Seitleman gave her the name of a Mensan attorney in Los Angeles, Herbert E. Selwyn. The estate took six years to wind up and she could not praise highly enough the expertise and devotion of the attorney and his associate. Once again, thanks to a Mensa contact.

The last story of Mensa friendship concerned E. Jimmee's nephew Paul. He was to spend some time in England during the autumn term (or as she put it, the fall semester), and decided to visit France first.

Arrangements had been made and tickets booked when Paul's travelling companion changed his plans. Being a somewhat shy person, not speaking French and never having travelled alone, Paul was very upset and anxious. His parents wished they knew someone – anyone – in France whom he could contact should he need assistance during his stay. His sister Jane tried to call some of her contacts in Paris, but it was August, the month when most Parisians leave the capital and head south. Another sister, Jill, was a member of Mensa and she had the bright idea of calling the Mensa Office. She was given the name of Mensa France's secretary in Versailles, François Adrien. The Adriens insisted Paul must stay with them. When Jill asked Madame Adrien if there was anything Paul could do for them in return, she answered, 'Just ask him to bring some crunchy peanut butter for our youngest daughter.'

Everyone in Paul's family was greatly relieved that this contact was made. Another big 'Thank you Mensa.' 'Don't speak to me about "causes" – Mensa's reason for being is to be,' was E. Jimmee's answer to the original question.

If there had ever been any lingering doubt in our minds about Mensa friendships it would have been dispelled in recent weeks, when David suffered a mild coronary and underwent by-pass surgery. Good wishes in the form of letters, cards, faxes, flowers and gifts poured in from all over the Mensa world. We were overwhelmed by people's concern. Irish Mensa held its Annual Gathering – the first one David had been unable to attend – and an enormous card arrived signed by everyone who had attended (instigated, I'm sure, by Paul McKinley, who kept in contact regularly). Every day of the eight-week wait for the operation was like a lifetime; the last weekend threatened to be interminable. Then, out of the blue, came a phone call from Ed Vincent enquiring whether we would like to have a visitor for coffee. He was at Dublin Airport having popped in from London on the off chance that David might feel like a chat. We were touched and astounded by his gentle kindness and had a battle royal to persuade him to stay with us for the two days. In his easy company the time sped by. Ed kept in touch throughout David's hospitalisation, and his warmth and encouragement were of enormous comfort to me. Is there anything more I can say about Mensa friendships? I can only echo E. Jimmee's comment and say, 'Thank you Mensa.'

CHAPTER 12

Folk tales

VICTOR SEREBRIAKOFF

It would be safe to say that no one in Mensa is better known than its Honorary President, Victor Serebriakoff. His involvement in the society is legendary, and it is not surprising that many of his Mensa friends were invited to his seventieth-birthday celebrations. On the great day he sat down to open his mail. Amid the multi-sized and many-coloured envelopes an official-looking British Mensa envelope claimed his attention; its contents were as follows:

Dear Mr Serebriakoff,

This is a difficult letter to write. The British Mensa Committee have been advised that whilst looking through the membership archives at

Wolverhampton your original IQ test papers were found. A member of the Wolverhampton Office staff checked the original IQ calculations and discovered that the IQ result relating to yourself was incorrect.

The last two digits were transposed and, when corrected, give a score which IS BELOW THE PASS RATE FOR MENSA MEMBERSHIP. Both British Mensa Chairman, Clive Sinclair, and the Executive Director, Harold Gale, have agreed that you hereby be advised that you are, therefore, not, and have not been at any time, a member of the Society. You are hereby requested to return all the documents in your possession that you have ever received from our organisation over the last thirty years.

According to BMC Treasurer, John Meredith, unfortunately the law and our Constitution do not allow any refund of subscriptions paid in the period.

We look forward to hearing from you soon and would mention that a large van will shortly visit your residence in order to repossess our documents.

Yours sincerely,

British Mensa Committee.

Victor's reply was succinct, handwritten and to the point.

Addressed to: The ex-Person Lally.

TAKE NOTE! By virtue of the power vested in me as HONORARY WORLD PRESIDENT OF MENSA and, pursuant to your last letter, BE IT KNOWN TO YOU that your membership of Mensa is TERMINATED FORTHWITH. You are also DISMISSED from your IMPROPER MEMBERSHIP of the following classes: THE HUMAN RACE, THE MAMMALIA, THE VERTEBRATES, THE EUKARYOTES AND THE CREATURA

You will, however, be permitted to remain IRISH.

Signed,

B. Brave. (Mensa President since previous incumbent was found out.)

Outside Person Serebriakoff sends his greetings and thanks for the birthday wishes.

Win Serebriakoff, knowing of the plot, had placed the envelope in a prominent position, stood back and waited. Despite this sabotage attempt, the birthday was celebrated according to plan.

SIR CLIVE SINCLAIR

Amongst its members Mensa has many famous people: scientists, authors, film stars, architects, television personalities, business people, Olympic gold medallists, boxers, members of parliament, members of pop groups and inventors. There are also unknown lawyers, nurses, bus conductors, farmers, engineers, homemakers, shop assistants and doctors. In short, Mensans come from every walk of life.

In the field of invention Sir Clive Sinclair is undoubtedly out on his own. It came as a great surprise to me to learn that after completing his secondary education at the age of seventeen, he became a technical journalist for four years.

In 1962 he founded his own company, Sinclair Radionics, in London and his first products included radio and amplifier kits which were sold by mail order. His reputation as a pioneer in the field of consumer electronics developed rapidly, particularly in miniaturisation.

On one of Clive's visits, David (who throws nothing away) produced a Sinclair transistor radio manufactured in the 1960s and long past its sell-by date and asked him if it could be repaired. Clive grinned and informed him the parts were 'out of stock at the moment'.

He moved to Cambridge and set a trend for many other high-technology companies. In 1972 the world's first pocket calculator, the 'Executive', was launched. It won numerous design awards and earned over £2.5 million in export revenue. The 'Cambridge' range took Clive to number one in the UK calculator market.

For the next couple of years the company invested heavily in research and development for new products, digital watches, a pocket television and instruments. In 1975 a low-cost digital multimeter was introduced. The 'Black Watch', a black-faced digital wristwatch which used a revolutionary new chip technology, was invented and marketed.

Additional funding was needed to support the final stages of the pocket-television project and this was sought from the National

Enterprise Board. Following a twelve-year investment programme of £0.5 million this became another 'world first' for Clive. A later version followed, the 'Microvision', selling for half the price of the first.

'The Man who Introduced Computers to the World', shrieked the newspaper headlines. The Sinclair ZX80 became the first personal computer to sell worldwide. It weighed just twelve ounces. This was soon followed by the more advanced ZX81 which won the Design Council award. One million units were sold and it would be interesting to learn how many of today's computer technicians started their careers on these compact machines. (We, of course, still have ours!) The next miracle of electronics was the flat-screen pocket television, a revolutionary idea using a new concept in optics.

Clive branched out into the world of publishing, and with Patrick Browne launched Sinclair Browne. For several years the firm sponsored the annual £5,000 'Sinclair Prize for Fiction' awarded for 'a novel which is not only of great literary merit but also of social and political significance'.

In 1983 Clive himself was the recipient of three awards; he became 'Computing person of the decade', 'Guardian young businessman of the year' and received a knighthood in the Queen's birthday honours list.

Blue-eyed boy, flavour of the month, darling of the press, Clive could not make a move without having a horde of eager reporters on his heels. But in 1985, which saw the launch of the Sinclair C5 electric tricycle, those same news hounds, forgetting all that had gone before, set about criticising the C5 at every opportunity. Despite the fact that it did not turn out to be a commercial success in the UK, it caught on in a number of overseas markets and models from the original production are still being sold at over twice the launch price. We saw models on show at the Smithsonian in Washington, the World Fair in Vancouver and in transport museums.

You cannot keep a good inventive genius down. Early in 1992 Clive's new and exciting invention hit the market, the 'Zike', a battery-operated bicycle. The amazingly neat battery is hidden along the machine's slim-line frame and it enables the cyclist to cruise along without effort, tackle inclines and slopes with ease and can slip in and out of traffic with a minimum of expended energy.

Clive now lives in London. His interests, apart from the obvious one, electronics, include poetry, music and mathematics. Over a period of years, David and I have come to know Clive as a kind, humorous, polite and generous friend – generous in both hospitality and spirit. When I told him about this book and asked him if he would write the foreword, he agreed without a second's hesitation, declaring that it sounded fun.

Clive's many inventions have taken him abroad on numerous occasions. After one business trip to the US he flew straight to Dublin for an annual general meeting of both British and Irish Mensa. At the informal dinner, jet lag could be staved off no longer and he fell asleep with his head on the table, at which point someone decided to shroud his head with a napkin. However, within fifteen minutes he had revived and was ready to enjoy the remainder of the evening. Unfortunately, there was a photographer there and his picture featured as a caption competition in *Mensa Magazine*. Clive, as usual, took it all in good part and helped judge the entries.

Mensa plays an important role in Clive's life despite his very busy schedule. Many of his friends are Mensans and he enjoys the social occasions, the gatherings and the black-tie dinners. As chairman of British Mensa, he is always a willing listener; he serves the organisation with care and fairness.

Mr Holmes of Baker Street

103,000 Mensans, 103,000 different people with differing opinions. Do not take fright – you will meet just a few of them. Some are long-serving members of committees around the globe, others are famous in their fields of endeavour and still others are known nationally or locally. The one thing they all have in common is the fact that they are Mensa folk.

It may be of interest to know that one of them, S. Holmes, is alive, well and living in Baker Street, London. Close by, lives his friend Dr Watson. Stewart Quentin Holmes, actor and journalist, changed his name by deed poll. A dedicated follower of Sherlock Holmes, he and his friend Dr Watson frequently entertain visitors at a nearby hotel. The famous detective and his faithful chronicler have a worldwide following and the two latter-day impersonators are hard to tell apart from the originals.

Stewart Holmes bears a strong resemblance to Gregory Peck and stood in for the star in the publicity for the film *The Million Pound Note*. The pay for his day's work did not contain as many zeros as Peck's would have had, but Stewart declared himself content.

After studying accountancy Stewart switched to journalism. He became acquainted with the Sherlock Holmes stories when learning Pitman shorthand and, joining forces with a childhood friend, Jerry Watson, then a photographer, they became the Holmes and Watson of Fleet Street.

Work petered out after a newspaper strike and Stewart Holmes went to Teheran as a BBC correspondent and stringer for half a dozen national newspapers, till the Shah, taking exception to an article he wrote, ordered his expulsion. His list of television and stage credits is most impressive; he has taken roles in operas and made commercials. He speaks three languages, French, German and Mandarin Chinese (accents and dialects to order!).

'Joining Mensa (in London) was one of the best things I ever did. I have attended many different events, met so many interesting people and had all sorts of adventures which do not happen in any other organisation,' declared Stewart.

As Stewart related his tales my note-taking ability failed yet again, but being a good-natured, kindly man he agreed to commit them to paper. The first one could be classed as a 'red-face' blooper.

Once upon a time there was an eating meeting in Putney. It was organised by a lady named Shirley (alas, no longer a member – and this is probably why). After dinner a long-standing member, Tony Hill, suggested that they all adjourn to his house for coffee (he lived close by the restaurant). Everyone was delighted and zoomed off in their cars to Tony's place. It was only after they had all arrived that someone asked 'Where's Shirley?' And it suddenly occurred to them that they had left her behind. Everyone had thought she was in somebody else's car, and no one noticed that she had gone to the loo when the coffee suggestion was made.

David Shenkin (at that time brain of Mensa) added a touch of hilarity when he suggested: 'Perhaps we should send her a card: "Wish you were here.'" Two members raced back to the restaurant, but there was no sign of Shirley. Later they called her home (she refused to answer), sent her flowers and letters of apology – to no avail. She left Mensa shortly afterwards, which Stewart said was a great shame, because she was a highly popular member and the success of her eating meetings was legendary.

There are few occasions when Stewart could be described as 'wet' but this was an exception to the rule. A group of Mensans went punting on the Cam. 'I knew that if anyone was going to fall into the water it would be me, so I took a change of clothing.'

Sure enough, he was right; they had just pushed away from the bank when he lost his grip on the punt pole, toppled over, and fell in. He was fished out and, inevitably, someone took a picture. 'My main memory', said Stewart, 'is of marching through the town, drenched to the skin (without anyone taking the slightest notice) until I reached my friend Bob's car (my clothes were in the boot).' Fortunately, they had parked outside a house with an enclosed entrance; he knocked at the door to ask whether he could change in the doorway.

'Nonsense, do come in,' said the generous occupier and provided Stewart with a towel so that he could dry and change comfortably. When he left, Stewart thanked him and said, 'If ever you are in London and fall into the Thames, feel free to call me and I shall be delighted to return the compliment.' Needless to say, he has not heard from the man.

Then there were the black-tie dinners which Stewart co-hosted with Julie Ward. 'We were fortunate in having the Royal Horseguards Hotel in London, next door to the National Liberal Club, where Victor Serebriakoff still organises his dinners.'

The hotel didn't charge for the hire of the excellent private room with which they provided them (complete with its own bar) and once dinner was served they were allowed to stay as long as they liked. The great thing about this event, Stewart said, was that diners were booking for the next dinner even before the current one had finished!

The great advantage of Mensa overseas is that it provides you with a band of ready-made friends wherever you go. In Honolulu the local secretary used to offer a seven-foot (yes, 7 ft) loaf of French bread at his Sunday meetings, and whenever you were hungry you just cut off a slice.

At a regional gathering in Dallas (I remember it well), Mensa took over the entire top floor of a major hotel. There was free food and drink all day, and if you helped behind the bar you earned Mensa dollars (they printed their own money) which could be spent downstairs in the casino or at the auction next door. It was all great fun.

Currently, the meetings which Stewart attends most are Ron Hendra's musical evenings at Wimbledon, which usually continue until three o'clock the following morning, and the occasional eating meetings organised by other members.

'I have often compared Mensa membership with Hong Kong,' Stewart observed. 'There's so much to do that one thing you can never be is bored.'

GABE WERBER

As Gabe Werber's life story unfolded I tried to visualise the setting in which he wrote it. We had visited Detroit (whilst our daughter Lynda was studying there) and had seen the Renaissance Center in which Gabe's offices are situated.

His life began in 1930, not in Detroit but in the Latin Quarter of Paris. His Russian parents were students at the Sorbonne, having made their way there from the University of Berlin. Gabe was brought up in Paris, where his father was a lawyer, Versailles and, because of the war, in Montpelier.

In 1941 the family arrived in the United States. Harlingen, Texas, in the lower Rio Grande valley, was to be their home. After graduating from high school at the age of fifteen, Gabe went on to the University of Texas where, three years later, he received his degree, Bachelor of Journalism. During that time he worked as a sportswriter and columnist.

New York beckoned and Gabe applied for jobs with the *New York Times* and *Herald Tribune*, only to be informed that they 'weren't hiring kids'. The next nine years were productive; he wrote scripts for documentary films, became executive director of a film society (often lecturing on films at the Museum of Modern Art and Hunter College), and a magazine researcher. He attended the Film Institute at City

College and New York's University Graduate School of Business Administration. In 1952 he married Barrie.

He then switched to public relations, becoming director of public relations and advertising in a company that went public. As he was having to deal constantly with lawyers and legal matters, he attended New York University's school of law in the evenings and was the year's 'best law note' in the evening division.

In 1962 Gabe left both his studies and his job; he and Barrie moved to Paris where for a year or more they 'lived the good life'. Back once more in the United States success followed success and in 1988 Gabe started his own public relations firm, Gabriel Werber & Associates. He admits it is growing nicely, far faster than he ever expected. He is also chairman of a direct marketing firm.

'Getting down to more important matters,' Gabe said, 'I have been a member of Mensa for twenty-eight years.' He joined as a way of meeting interesting and stimulating minds and his hopes have been more than fully realised. It might be an easier task to list the committee positions in American Mensa which Gabe has not held. His resignation (or sabbatical?) was the cause of much regret and also some hilarity as the photograph which appeared in the *Bulletin* with his name under it was of an attractive lady with long, brown hair. Gabe intends to remain a very active member of the society and continues to serve International Mensa as a wise and important national representative for his country.

As readers of the *Bulletin* we were familiar with Gabe's name. David's first meeting with him was in Rome and he immediately took to his company and sense of humour. This urbane man has very definite likes and dislikes. The dislikes are few: humourless, intolerant people with no sense of perspective; people who hurt other people; mushrooms, oysters and clams (oyster mushrooms must be total anathema); cocktail parties, and dinner parties for more than four people. He certainly shows no unwillingness to join the large tables of diners at Mensa gatherings.

His list of likes is long and includes Sundays; doing things with his family (which can be difficult with his son usually in Texas and his daughter at school); being with close friends; political and philosophical discussions; lying in the sand on tropical beaches; visiting museums and art galleries; collecting art (mostly abstract); quick-minded people;

people with a civilised outlook, a sense of humour, tolerance and compassion; music, theatre, ballet, contemporary dance and opera; the cinema and reading (Malraux, Gide, Camus, Saint Exupéry, S.J. Perelman).

IAN HADLEY

Ian Hadley went to sea – not in a beautiful pea-green boat but in a ship of the British Merchant Navy. Born in Oldham, England, in 1944 and raised in Glasgow, Ian admitted with a grin that he had scored 'extraordinarily high' in an IQ test taken by all ten-year-olds in school at that time and that his education had been plain sailing.

Like most Glaswegians he entered the shipping industry; he both built ships and sailed in them. After qualifying as an electrical draughtsman and working on Clydeside, he grew restless and walked away to sea. After circling the globe a number of times he returned to Glasgow and rediscovered his land legs. He applied to join the newly opened Honeywell company and after putting him through a barrage of tests they suggested that the computer development test centre would be the right place for him.

Ian joined Mensa for the first time in the mid-sixties, teased into taking the test by a friend who was part of the 'school intelligentsia clique'. 'I really knew nothing about Mensa at that time but who could resist a challenge like that?' Ian said.

He spent the next few years learning about digital computers and ended up as 'trouble shooter, northern Europe'. His expertise in the field of computer hardware took him to many countries in Europe and eventually to Australia. In 1972, while living in Melbourne, Ian joined Australian Mensa as he felt the need for kindred spirits.

Ian's interest turned to software; he left Honeywell and trained as a systems programmer. He became involved in a small organisation which provided data-processing services to libraries. Building the hardware, writing the software and selling the product kept him busy for some years. Eventually he was approached by a fellow Mensan from Bristol, who was building up a management consultancy in Australia. The transition was painless and Ian started specialising in computer fraud as well as computer measurement, both fairly high-tech aspects of the computer business.

This focus on performance measurement led to the publication of a monograph on the subject, co-written by Ian and fellow Mensan Roger Buoy, which was published in the late seventies and got on to the required-reading list of Deakin University in Geelong, Victoria. Computer-related fraud was also gaining a much higher profile at this time.

An interest in crime eventually led to Ian's becoming consultant to the New South Wales fraud squad, and adviser to the director general of security for the Federal Attorney General of Australia. By this time he had formed his own consultancy and was practising and lecturing throughout Australia and Asia.

Inevitably Ian spent a considerable amount of time in Asia. 'In Western Australia', he pointed out, 'you are closer to Singapore than you are to Sydney.' He visited Papua New Guinea, Hong Kong, Jakarta, Bali, Singapore and Kuala Lumpur. His lecture stops lasted three or four days and, in some of the countries, life was harsh and totally different from that of the Western world.

In some countries a particular kind of herbal cigarette is popular. These are perfectly legal and are sold openly be vendors on bicycles who weave their way in and out of the teeming traffic. One night Ian was invited to the home of a business associate and the lady of the house appeared to tell him she had inadvertently knocked one of the vendors from his bicycle and killed him. She said, quite indignantly, that might have had to spend an evening, maybe even the whole night, in police custody had not her father located the deceased's family, negotiated a price and secured her freedom by paying it. The only role of the police in the affair had been only to ensure that all parties agreed amicably on a price. That in her eyes was the end of the matter. There was still a note of disbelief in Ian's voice as he repeated this story which happened quite a long time ago.

By the late seventies, the computers and computing were changing at an ever accelerating pace. Stephen Jobs and Steve Wozniak had started a revolution by assembling the first Apple computer in their garage. It was rejected by Wozniak's employer, Hewlett Packard, as not commercial.

Clive Sinclair was doing wondrous things with a hand-held computer called a Spectrum and even IBM had decided that small is better. Ian's old friend and fellow Mensan, Roger Buoy, had returned to the USA by 1980 and was in the process of forming a company which would develop and publish educational and game software for the new consumer market. He invited Ian to join the venture and so Ian left Australia for Chicago, Illinois in the very cold winter of 1984.

The vagaries of the consumer software market made the following five years very eventful and interesting – roller coasters can give a smoother ride. Ian grew disillusioned, left this industry and returned to management consultancy, forming a new company based in Illinois. He concentrated on the business of relocating corporations, mostly from urban centres, in country and suburban locations. In addition, a return to computer-related fraud and security had him formulating policy and setting out protection measures for some fairly well-known and established Wall Street clients.

During this time, however, his affection for computer games did not wither. At home in the evenings and at weekends he wrote and rewrote some classic games for Apple, Amiga and Macintosh computers. In the summer of 1984 he was asked to consider setting up a computer gaming company in Ireland. The Californian company, Cinemaware, intended to establish a development facility in Dublin under the auspices of the Industrial Development Authority and needed a managing director who understood the business. In January 1990 Ian moved to Dublin.

Arriving in Ireland six months ahead of his family he felt the need for some good company, and where better to turn than to Mensa? He telephoned the Irish Mensa office and David suggested that he come along to the first-Thursday-of-the-month meeting. He did, and Irish Mensa became number three on his Mensa list. Ian has become a popular and valued addition to the group.

Cinemaware Inc. went under in the recession and with it the Irish subsidiary. Undaunted, Ian formed his own company from the ashes, sought and found a UK partner in Gremlin Graphics Software and formed Gremlin Graphics (Ireland) Ltd. They are about to publish their first product for IBM and Amiga computers. It is an adventure game based on the movie *Plan 9 from Outer Space*, which was the worst movie ever made, so bad that it won the Golden Turkey Award. It has a huge cult following. 'We have incorporated around two minutes of actual film footage in the product', Ian said, 'which is something of a first for leisure software. The compression needed is huge.' The company is planning to focus on CD-based products in order to take advantage of the next revolution in computing which, in Ian's opinion, will be multi-media productions.

Ian met and married Christine in 1967. They have a son Stephen and a daughter Caroline, both of whom are Mensa material, according to Ian. 'Why aren't they members?' I asked (in my role of Mensa's answer to Billy Graham). 'Probably because their Dad is a member,' said Ian with a grin. We hope that this friendly, interesting and good-humoured man, who has survived two heart attacks, will now stop his wanderings and give up his career as a join-again Mensan.

A LIFE OF JOY

'Life is magic,' said Joy Peach. Her articles in Mensa publications are always interesting, amusing and informative, and this prompted me to telephone and ask if she would be willing to write a profile of herself. She agreed readily, but said, 'I'll have to relate it verbally' Joy is a born writer, so it was obvious that she was suffering from damage to either her hand or her typewriter. The record holder for conclusion-jumping could not have been further from the amazing truth.

Despite her talent and the fact that she contributed to many Mensa publications, to national newspapers such as the *Guardian* and the *Observer* and to several prestigious journals, Joy was unable to make a living from her writing. A government grant allowed her to pursue her career but it remained an uphill struggle. After the grant had run out and considerable time had passed, she reluctantly applied for social security. All that was necessary in order for her to receive her benefit was her signature on a document stating that she was a failed writer and that she would never write anything again. Joy reasoned that if she were permitted to continue to write, and her writing proved successful, she would cease to be a burden on the state. This logic fell on deaf ears and, with the warning ringing in her brain that she must not write as much as a shopping list, the disbelieving Joy accepted her fate. (Her case was taken up by the Society of Authors and, after a long fight, she won the right to continue trying to wrest a living out of her word processor.

Joy was not a believer in IQ tests; in fact, she went so far as to say, 'If I had thought about it at all, the very idea of Mensa would have given me the willies.' However, like many others, every time she saw one of the brain teasers Mensa use as publicity she would 'have a bash at it, just for fun'. A couple of years ago, on a whim, she applied for the self-administered test and, having returned it to Wolverhampton, forgot all about it. Ten days later a letter arrived inviting her to take the supervised test, the results of which elicited the usual reaction, 'It must be a mistake.'

Born in 1933 under the sign of Sagittarius Joy was the second child and eldest daughter in a family of seven, three boys and four girls. All of them, apart from her, she thought, were brilliant and successful. Her childhood was clouded by illness. From infancy she suffered from severe epilepsy and hardly ever managed a full week at school until the age of twelve, when she was cured (she was told) by the laying on of hands. Up till then she had been having four or five major fits a week, but after that there was never a whisper of trouble. (Two of her children are epileptic, both of them exceedingly bright – one has just gained a doctorate in ornithology.)

Joy wanted to make three points about her cure. The first was that she felt her life after it had been a bonus – both the magic and the pain. At the time she was cured her parents were in the process of applying for a place for her in the first Camphill Village, a community offering lifelong shelter to the handicapped.

Her second point was that it was not until she was well into her thirties that it dawned on her that, whilst other people could remember back to their days at infant school and earlier, her memory went no further back than her early teens. She may have looked like a grown woman as she walked up the aisle but, she said, 'To all intents and purposes this bride was a dopey ten-year-old. No wonder the marriage failed.'

It is now accepted that our phobias and inhibitions mostly originate in our formative years. The wise and loving upbringing her parents lavished on their large family made not the slightest impression on Joy, unlike her achieving siblings; she was the odd one out, the black sheep, the wild card, the disappointment. On the other hand, she seemed to have missed out on those crippling handicaps, guilt and regret, which was just as well, as her life since her schooldays had been little more than a catalogue of disasters.

After what she described as 'a revolting period in the lower sixth form at school', she got a job as a kitchen maid at Eton College. 'I must have been one of the very few domestic servants who spent their afternoons off taking Greek coaching from the house master,' said Joy.

From there she went to Lausanne, where she spent twelve painful months 'au pairing' – a euphemism for slavery, she soon discovered. She returned home, battered literally and psychologically, and somehow allowed herself to be persuaded to take a teacher-training course.

'Oh my stars! Talk about disaster! I could not impose order on the classes of forty or more street-wise teenagers, let alone maintain it,' Joy said. In those days you had to teach for at least two years after qual-ifying or repay your college fees and grant (such as it was) in full. She struggled through her probationary year with a class of mixed juniors in the backwoods of Warwickshire, towards the end of which the chief educational officer sent for her. He did not present her with a certificate of competence but advised her – and here she noted a hint of hysteria in his demeanour – to give up teaching and return to domestic service.

This she promptly did and married her first boyfriend. This was another ghastly mistake. Her husband was the only person she came across in those days who knew his IQ (he must have been tested for National Service). 'Haven't I done well?' he used to say as he progressed up the teaching ladder. 'And me with an IQ of 112.'

When Joy finally extricated herself from wedlock she found that she was still incapable of holding down a teaching job despite having four children of her own and the wisdom of her years. She flitted half-heartedly from one soul-destroying job to the next.

In 1980, for the first time in her life, Joy found herself a wonderful position. She became assistant archivist in the County Record Office, a job in which she was entirely comfortable. 'Bliss!' she said. 'They actually paid me to rummage quietly through boxes of documents, faded, fragile, fascinating; to catalogue and index them; to create order out of chaos. I experienced job satisfaction.'

But not for long. In 1986, when the inevitable cut-backs hit the archives, someone was for the chop and, as last in and an unqualified part-timer to boot, it was Joy. She found herself redundant without redundancy payment, unemployed but not entitled to unemployment benefit. Luckily, a maintenance of sorts from her ex-husband helped a little but it did not go very far even in those days, as nearly half of it was immediately gobbled up by the mortgage.

For the next three months she applied for 'every darn job that was advertised', from library assistant to office cleaner, but it soon became clear that she was unemployable. 'Smarten yourself up,' her parents advised. 'Do something about that hair.' 'They didn't realise I wasn't even getting as far as an interview.'

Limp from malnutrition and anxiety, and knowing that her maintenance cheque could be reduced the minute her youngest child left university, Joy tidied the house ('God! what fools we women are!'), put her last will and testament on the kitchen table and tottered down to the bridge spanning the railway tracks. She was leaning over the parapet waiting to throw herself under the 12.06 (Bournemouth to Waterloo), when it dawned on her that at least her children would benefit from her death. 'Our humble terraced cottage in well-heeled Winchester, an hour from London, must be worth a bob or two.'

Just as the train roared into sight, it occurred to her that if her children could benefit from the sale of the house, so could she. 'I could sell it, find something similar up North for half the price, invest the difference and live on the interest. Eureka!' In her excitement she nearly tumbled under the express as it shot through the station below her but, fortunately, she had managed to impale herself on the railings and, five minutes later, with torn jeans, a bleeding ankle and the light of battle in her eye, she had selected an estate agent and set in motion the chain of events which was to lead to a new life in Whitby – in a beautiful old cottage in this quaint Yorkshire fishing port. As a woman of substance? No. *En route* she fell into the hands of an unscrupulous builder who left her penniless. Currently she is scraping along on income support while lawyers wrangle over the compensation. 'Thank God for Legal Aid!' Joy said.

'I am afraid I can't afford to take your supervised test,' Joy wrote to Mensa. She could not even afford the bus fare to Middlesbrough, the nearest test centre, let alone meet the cost of an overnight stay. 'We can offer some financial assistance in cases such as yours,' they wrote back. 'I crawled round to ask my long-suffering bank manager to lend me £40 for the expedition. This perhaps showed the first glimmer of intelligence. By eliminating the poverty-related stress from my life, I could ensure that I did myself justice – for the test day at least.'

She booked herself into a three-star hotel and, after treating herself to an excellent ham salad and arranging to be called with a tray of tea at 4.30 p.m., she retired to her room for a luxurious bath and slept the afternoon away. When the taxi arrived to take her to the test centre at 6.30 ('I was really into this executive life style, as you can see!'), she was calm, confident and clear-headed.

And then the results came through. After a lifetime of failure and frustration, poverty and rejection, they told her ('Don't laugh,' she said) that with an IQ of 160 she qualified, and easily, to join the exalted ranks of Mensa.

'Ludicrous, isn't it, but in a funny way I have to admit that this silly little figure on the silly little certificate has made a difference.' Suddenly she felt strong, credible, fearless. It was like having a healthy bank balance (she imagined) – or *any* bank balance for that matter. She had become sound, respectable, of measurable worth.

When the daily batch of rejection slips from editors and publishers plops through the letter box she no longer collapses in despair. Nowadays she is able to scoop them up without a qualm and redirect them without delay.

Joy has got her name on to the register of Speakers Finders Agency in Peterborough ('at a starting rate of £125 per talk plus expenses – real money, what!'). She has finished her fourth unpublished novel and 'It's good, though I sez it myself.' She is working on a book about her very special system of reading the tarot with the help of a pendulum, and has not yet found a publisher for this either.

After a good many agonising years she has finally found the strength to send her distinguished but cold-blooded lover packing. She is no longer prepared to accept second best. Financially things are as dodgy as ever. 'As I talk to you I am expecting to have my cottage repossessed by the bank, but apart from that, life is sparkling with colour, drama and – sorry, no other word will do – love.' Her children are all happily launched. They have turned out loving, strong, intelligent and creative in spite of their dismal start in life – the broken marriage syndrome. Joy is constantly amazed to have survived all those years of motherhood and now to be wallowing in blissful solitude.

'The third point?' I asked. 'It's my interest in mysteries, in the as yet inexplicable: the tarot, pendulum power, colour analysis and "all that stuff" – all strongly connected to the laying on of hands that made such a difference to my life. I've had to concede that "there are more things in heaven and earth Horatio ...", more things than even the brightest intellect can explain away.'

'Funny how things turn out, isn't it? Funny what a difference an IQ score can make to your self-respect. I have a little chuckle about it sometimes as I queue up to cash my income support giro on a Friday.'

VELMA JEREMIAH

Velma Jeremiah is one of the few Americans that I have met who are living in the state in which they were born – Oregon in Velma's case. She is also one of the few people to begin a career as a stand-up comedian after her retirement.

She zipped through high school in just two years and decided she wanted to be an architect. She worked for a year in order to earn money for her education but it was insufficient and she was forced to drop out. During World War II Velma secured a job as a cryptographer in Alaska. Whilst there she met and married a sailor and they had a son, Dale. Her marriage eventually broke up and she supported herself and her son by doing secretarial work and rose to the position of chief executive secretary in a company providing forestry products.

Velma, however, was determined to acquire credentials that no one could ignore and had set her sights on a career that promised financial reward; she chose law. She had many hurdles to jump. Without a first degree – but with a lot of determination – she took an exam which proved her IQ was in the top two per cent of the required result. She entered the Northwestern School of Law at Lewis and Clark College and passed a two-year college equivalency exam, working by day and taking classes at night.

'Finding a law firm that wanted a middle-aged female attorney wasn't easy,' Velma said. It took a year before she was hired by a firm in Portland, Oregon. She loved law and her hard work and dedication eventually earned her a partnership.

It was whilst working as a partner in this firm that she received a very pleasant surprise bonus. She had done some legal work for a friend and fellow Mensan, John Hackenbruck, and sent him a bill. He telephoned – Velma was convinced it was to complain about the cost – but what he said was, 'I just got your bill, counselor. You have vastly undercharged me for an excellent piece of work.' 'Lawyers don't get phone calls like that too often,' Velma stressed. She assured him that the fee was correct and John rang off telling Velma that he would 'get even with her somehow'.

Months later, while attending an American Mensa annual gathering, Velma ran into Margot Seitleman (then executive director of American Mensa) who told her that she had something for her which 'a friend' had asked Margot to give her. It was a life membership card. 'John couldn't have chosen a better gift,' said Velma. 'Sadly, he's dead now, but every year when I receive my new life member's card, I think of him.'

Velma retired in 1986. She began to feel depressed; life seemed to hold no more challenges. Things changed, however, in the spring of 1989 when she read of a stand-up comedy class. It was tough going gaining the confidence to face an audience, but Velma has gone from strength to strength. No quiet, discreet, genteel clubs for this determined lady, she has appeared in comedy clubs before rowdy audiences, and her ambition is to become good enough to get on to a late night talk show or to entertain on a cruise ship.

Comedy is just one of Velma's many interests; she also enjoys travel, Nordic skiing, hiking – after retiring in 1986 she went trekking in Nepal – white-water river running, reading and last, but definitely not least, Mensa – whose current International Chairman she is. In Velma's opinion, 'Age is a laughing matter.'

MENSA AND MAMMOTHS

Jean Auel first learned of Mensa in the early 1960s through an article in *Life Magazine*. Born in Chicago, Illinois, Jean was married at eighteen and had had five children by the age of twenty-five. She had reached a stage when she wanted to open up her life, so she sent for the test. The article mentioned that by paying a small fee one could not only take an IQ test but also obtain the scores. 'I took the test in order to find out for myself if I were smart enough to go to college,' Jean wrote. After she achieved the scores she received a letter from the secretary of the local chapter of Mensa in Oregon inviting her to a gathering. She decided to go simply out of curiosity. 'Approaching with a certain amount of trepidation, and dragging my husband along with me,' Jean said, 'I attended my first meeting and found a host of people with whom I immediately felt comfortable.' To this day some of her best friends are people she met in the early days of Mensa.

In 1976, armed with a Master's degree in business, Jean gave up her career as credit manager for an electronics company and began to write. *The Clan of the Cave Bear, The Valley of Horses, The Mammoth-Hunters* and *The Plains of Passage* are best sellers worldwide. Her first novel, *The Clan of the Cave Bear*, took three years to research and write. She worked from fourteen to sixteen hours a day, seven days a week and the book was praised not only for its story but also for the detailed research that had gone into it. It was a smash hit.

An Honorary Vice-President of Mensa, Jean regrets that she is not as active in the local Mensa group as she once was. 'Writing takes so much time.' The demands of publishers, both American and foreign, as well as the disciplines she imposes on herself for accurate research leave her with hardly any time to spend with family and friends. 'I miss those old days of getting to know Mensa, and will always feel a warmth for the organisation.'

A LONG STRETCH

Not everyone has the freedom of choice or movement which most people take for granted. Richard Z. White, as I shall call him, left home at fifteen years of age and from then on things went seriously wrong. Unlike a lot of young people in that position the more difficult his problems became the harder he worked, until work became an obsession. Suffering from mental, physical and emotional exhaustion he began to drink and that, coupled with medication, led him to commit murder. Far from being planned, it was an act of emotional blindness during which, for that brief moment, reason and morality ceased to exist. Richard made no attempt to evade the law.

His victim was a stranger, a fact which, more than any other, has haunted him throughout his years of confinement. Having served fifteen years of his life sentence he is convinced that he is neither criminally minded nor amoral but, for the sake of the family of the victim, he did not wish to enlarge on the subject. His guilt and the loneliness of life in prison have been the two most difficult things to bear.

Despite all obstacles and continuous noise Richard has used his ability and intelligence. He took an Open University arts foundation course, working by day at his prison job and studying at night in his cell. Having left school at the age of fifteen he had no qualifications and was barely able to spell. He modestly admitted to attaining a 2.1 degree in literature.

He went on to acquire basic skills in computing and typing, started to learn French, play bridge and he reads widely. He has helped produce concerts in the prison and learned to paint. After some years he felt he had done all that he could do and his motivation flagged. At the recommendation of a psychiatrist he applied to take the Mensa test and his success in achieving the required standard gave him a great boost. Unable to attend meetings, he focused his attention on the special interest groups, writing for the newsletters and contributing to the magazines. Mensa has become a welcome new interest for him and some of its members visit him from time to time. He has helped other inmates with study, essays and the writing of letters.

As Richard pointed out, this may sound like a busy and productive way of life, but weeks may go by when boredom and apathy get on top of him. Meditation and yoga help him, and although he does not practise either on a daily basis, he does find them effective in times of anxiety, apathy and stress.

Richard has kept various pets over the years, and has currently adopted, or been adopted by, a family of pigeons numbering ten in all. They have very definite personalities and pretend no shyness when it comes to sharing his rations. He has paired them off into couples and named them all, and he enjoys their amusing antics. One cheeky bird perches on his bed as if he owned it (which is all right with Richard as this one is his favourite) while another pops her head round the window before flying in and perching.

I asked Richard if he felt there was any positive side to his years of imprisonment and he said he thought there was none. However, in the light of his achievements, I am sure few would agree with him. He did express the hope that the pain of his years of confinement had given him some wisdom.

THE NUMBERS GIRL

Tools down – it's *Countdown*. Each weekday, for several months a year, everything in the house stops at 4.30 while we watch this riveting and highly competitive television quiz show.

Carol Vorderman, the show's mathematical expert, holds a Master's degree in engineering from Cambridge University. After graduating at the age of twenty, Carol was taken on as a management trainee by Christian Salveson; her jobs included driving a fork-lift truck, supervising the packaging of frozen peas and working for the housing division. Then she was head-hunted by the giant Tandy Corporation and sold computers in Leeds until the day her mother saw an article in the *Yorkshire Evening Post* under the headline 'Beauty and brains wanted' which said that the producer of *Countdown* was looking for a girl to control the 'numbers' section of the game.

Two contestants compete against each other in this game which consists of six randomly-selected numbers. On a display table four numbers – 25, 50, 75 and 100 are concealed. The rest of the hidden numbers range from 1 to 10. The contestant selects six of the numerical cards (usually one large number and five small ones) which are then displayed in slots, a button is pressed and a random number – not exceeding 999 – appears. Contestants are then allotted 30 seconds to attempt to reach the random number using the six selected numbers once only and using any acceptable mathematical method(s). The 'numbers girl' not only draws and displays the number cards as they are selected by the contestants but also has the task of showing how the target could have been achieved on the many instances when the contestants are unsuccessful.

Despite receiving over 2,000 applications for the position the producer did not find the right girl for the programme. Carol did not think she stood a chance but her mother wrote a letter and, by the time Carol was interviewed, more than 3,000 applications had been received. She was selected and became the 'numbers girl'. Carol has to solve the mathematical problems in the same thirty seconds as the competitors and her mathematical genius rarely lets her down.

The other part of the quiz show, the word section which involves try-ing to make the longest word out of nine randomly-selected letters, was originally presented by another girl, a Mensa member, Denise. A reporter mistakenly wrote that it was Carol who was the Mensan. She felt, under the circumstances, that she should become a member and had no difficulty in passing the test. She went on to serve on the British Mensa committee.

The programme moved from regional television to Channel 4 and Carol, at the tender age of twenty-one, became the first woman to appear on the newly-launched Channel 4. The show has a dedicated audience and is always high in the ratings; it has been booked for a further five years. Not surprisingly there are a lot of Mensans among the competitors and on one particular day both contestants were members of the society. Carol now presents both the letters and the numbers sections of the game and enjoys exchanging teasing badinage with the host of the show, Richard Whiteley, quick-thinking master of the most dreadful puns.

Carol accepts with amused resignation that she will always be known first and foremost for her appearances on *Countdown*. As charming as she is pretty, Carol made time in her busy schedule to talk to me about her great interest in education. 'Education takes 120 per cent of my time,' Carol said. Since becoming resident mathematician on the programme Carol's television career has expanded and she is totally committed to popularising numeracy and science via the media.

She co-presented, with Professor Ian Fells, two series of *Take Nobody's Word for It* (a BBC science series which has won three awards). It was during this series that Carol made her first trip to Holland. This was particularly interesting for her as she is half Welsh/half Dutch. Whilst filming there she was also able to research information about her great-grandfather, Dr A. G. Vorderman, an inspector-general in the Dutch East Indies (now Indonesia) who helped to discover the cure for beri-beri. Author of several books on the bird life and plants of the islands, he has two butterflies named after him and was awarded the highest honours of the Netherlands.

Carol has presented the BBC's successful *Software Show* and various series including *A Way with Numbers, Sum Chance, So We Bought a Computer, Power Base, Circuit Training, Wide-awake Club, WAC '90, Kid's Café, Sounds Good, Pick of the Week, Carwise, Music on TV*. She has appeared as a guest celebrity on numerous shows including *Jim'll Fix It* hosted by Sir James (Jimmy) Savile, another Mensan.

In *A Way with Numbers* she presents a series of twenty programmes dealing with adult numeracy. A new series of *How!* (ITV's longest-running children's programme) is being prepared. *Ask Carol* and *Carol's Fablab* are another two of her presentations. She has written two books of science experiments for young children, *Dirty, Loud and Brilliant* and *Dirty, Loud and Brilliant Too*. Her own production, *The Vorderman Report*, was transmitted on Yorkshire TV.

Carol's latest painless teaching aids are videotapes for ten- to sixteen-year-olds covering the mathematics and English on the National Curriculum. They have been a huge success. For the six to ten age group, *Video Class Times Tables* is proving to be a best seller. She has had her own musical scores written for the videos, with fifty minutes of pop music from rap to Madonna-style, to heavy rock and the sounds of the sixties (a series of eleven videos). 'It is enormously rewarding when parents of three-year-olds tell me the youngsters have mastered all their tables, aided by these videos,' says Carol. She's one terrific lady, that *Countdown* girl!

PETER DOWD

Undoubtedly one of the most enjoyable series of letters I have received was from Peter Dowd, a member of Irish Mensa. My first contact with Peter was a letter telling me that, when teaching at an international summer school in England last year, he ended each day's classes with a puzzle from one of my books. One pupil, who was invariably first with the answers (always correct), has now, through the book, become a member of International Mensa.

In his next letter he wished me luck with this book and offered his help with it. I was delighted to accept and asked him to supply a profile. I apologised for the brevity of my letter. His reply began, 'So you're panicking nicely, are you? Good, good.' And there followed what he modestly referred to as a lowly profile.

Peter took the supervised Mensa test in 1986, panicking all the way through it (so, I'm not the only one!). He passed and attended his first meeting soon after. There he discovered that he got on well with these alleged oddballs. Peter said that he had always thought that he was weird but, at last, discovered that he was quite normal.

At the age of nineteen he had joined the civil service and soon realised that this was a big mistake. When he was twenty-two he discovered he had an uncanny knack with languages and has been either 'teaching them' or 'learning them' ever since. Five years later he left the civil service and went to Copenhagen to look after the secretary of Denmark Mensa's cat while he (the secretary) was on holiday in the United States. This trip to Denmark was supposed to last a fortnight; two years later Peter returned to Ireland.

In his time Peter has been: a bingo caller, tour guide, chamber maid, hotel receptionist, rye-bread baker, shop assistant. Now, at the age of thirty, he is training to be a chef. 'Mensa has done a lot for me,' he says, 'but the main thing it did was to give me the kick in the pants I needed to change my life-style/way of living – four times so far. Psychologically Mensa has shown me that life is indeed what you make it.'

My very short reply to his letter consisted of five, four-word sentences thanking him and explaining that time was running short. 'Cheers, Anne. *Loved* the letter – must be the shortest, most concise letter I've ever had,' Peter wrote. He went on to say that the shortest and best letter ever was written by Alexander Dumas to his publisher. Its total contents – '?'. The reply was just as informative and concise – '!'. Beat that, instructed Peter. I did. My response was carefully centred on a large sheet of blank paper – '.'!

Peter, LocSec for Irish Mensa's western region, is off to Norway to visit Mensa friends and broaden his horizons even more. One of his many Mensa interests is a survey he instigated on twin members. Two sets in British Mensa and one pair in American Mensa responded. In all cases they had done the tests independently of each other and obtained similar scores. This experiment was sparked off by his own twin brother taking the home test some years after Peter and getting exactly the same score. (He did not go on to take the supervised test, Peter said; his wife wouldn't let him.)

The latest communication arrived two weeks ago via David, following an Irish Mensa committee meeting (Peter is an elected member). Not another letter, but a wonderful Peter-made dill and onion loaf, one of his continental specialities. I know nothing of Peter's teaching abilities but as a baker he is a winner.

VIVIENNE SMITH – OR NAKED LUNCH

There was a young lady from Reading ... Vivienne Smith had arranged for another member to give her a lift to a meeting and a meal at his home before it. She arrived and rang the bell. The door was opened by her host who was stark naked. Thinking he must just have had a bath and forgotten his towel, she coolly followed him inside and sat down on the couch. He excused himself and left the room, returning with a tray of drinks, but not a stitch of clothing. Vivienne inspected the walls, the paintings, the pattern on the wallpaper and the carpet. A fluttering cobweb in one corner of the room was riveting. Turning her attention to her host she studied his eyebrows. The right one was composed of 624 hairs, the left one had six fewer. When he announced that dinner was ready Vivienne was delighted, at least now she would be able to look in the direction of her host. She followed him into another room where he politely seated her at a glass-topped table. 'If frankfurters were on the menu,' Vivienne said, 'I was leaving, lift or no lift!'

CAROL BROWN, BALLAD OF A SQUARE PEG

Carol Brown expressed reservations about being a member of Mensa. She had on occasion submitted letters and poetry to the magazine but to no avail. She did not attend meetings and felt somewhat isolated. By nature she is a cheerful mother-of-six and, despite having impaired sight, her myriad interests include tapestry work, painting, gardening, puzzles, writing and poetry. Poetry is her favourite and she enclosed this poem with her letter.

Square peg

I'm feeling confused about being in Mensa,
     It isn't so easy up here 'at the top'
To say my IQ is one hundred and fifty
     I'm feeling inadequate, hurt and a flop.

No one has rung me to offer positions
     That bring in the shekels or promise prestige
I'm still potting plants, to the elbow in compost
     Or out on the standing-ground pulling out weeds.

I always suspected I was a bit brighter
     Than Madgie my neighbour or Norman at work
But now that I've proved it and got it in writing
     They're making me feel a bit of a jerk.

I didn't expect to be toasted or feted
     Or hit the front page with my name up in lights

Nor did I expect *University Challenge*
 With sniggers and boos if I don't get it right.

I refrained from making a public announcement,
 Sporting a tee-shirt or wearing a badge,
I just wanted to shine in my own little corner,
 Not get daily baiting from Norman and Madge.

Seeking a soul-mate for some consolation,
 I scour the letters in my Mensa mag.
The FMs and MMs are all under thirty
 I'm sure they would find me a bit of a drag.

They're all in computers or nuclear physics
 They're MAs or BAs, with honours of course.
Or they're fun-seeking, sun-seeking, ever-so-clever
 With money to squander and plenty of sauce.

I'm feeling inadequate 'cos I am in Mensa.
 Should I be out there being crucial and wise?
Heading a think-tank, astounding the masses,
 Or standing in line for a Pulitzer prize.

But I'm happy to stay caning up the clematis,
 Weeding the hebes or pruning the trees,
Freezing in winter, scorching in summer,
 At one with the world like the birds and the bees.

Is there anyone out there, happily knitting,
 Watching *Knot's Landing* or feeding a pig?
A typist, a storeman, an out-of-work doorman,
 Let's all get together and start our own SIG.

Start your own SIG! When I replied to her letter I suggested that several of the special interest groups (SIGs) would take her out of the isolation she so obviously felt. I was both red-faced and pleased when she wrote back to say that she had needed the kick in the pants that I had delivered and that she had applied to five of the groups.

MENSA AND ME

Having 'pegged out' on the clothes line the lives of a number of Mensans, it seems only fair to give my own an airing. I was born in Manchester (at a date still to be decided) and the family moved to Dublin when I was two years old. I began my schooling at the age of four and it was heaven. I took to it like a duck to water, reading, writing and arithmetic, but by far my favourite subject was Irish. I now think it was probably the beautiful script, long since vanished, that appealed to me more than the language.

Points were awarded each week for schoolwork and an honour card was given to the child with top marks. Those blue-edged cards were the joy of my life, and there were not too many Fridays when I returned home without one. In those days it was safe for children to go out, and several of us walked the two miles to school and back, stopping on the way for bags of sweets or bars of some tooth-rotting sugary confection whilst avoiding some of the spine-chilling terrors which children enjoy so much.

Our particular terrors were three people, Mad Mary, Forty Coats and Bang-Bang. We knew for a fact that Mad Mary, if she caught us, would eat us for tea, just like all the other children she had devoured. The poor deranged woman yelled at any passer-by but was harmless. We ran like the wind down any street in which she appeared, our hearts barely finding room in our chocolate-crowded mouths. It does not need Mensan intelligence to work out the reason for Forty Coats' nickname. Layer upon layer of coats made him look like a giant to us. He shuffled and muttered his way along the roads and our spines tingled with fear as we approached him and then with relief as we passed him. He too was harmless. Bang-Bang was not quite as alarming as the other two. He mainly confined his activities to the buses or trams. He would hop on to the back and, clinging to the hand rail, would 'shoot' every citizen in sight with cries of 'Bang! Bang!' I can see now that he was just some harmless fellow who imagined he was John Wayne, hanging out of the back of a beleaguered stage-coach.

I took to crime at a tender age. My friend Olive (a hardened criminal aged six) and I stole two red apples from an orchard near our homes. These apples were so huge that they were almost ready to drop off the tree. We climbed the orchard wall and reached out for the forbidden fruit; flushed with success we sauntered home down the lane. Just as we were rubbing the juicy spoils on our sleeves a bellow stopped us in our tracks. A very angry farmer threatened to call the police. Olive reached home first, and in any case she was not nearly as frightened as I was as she had often 'shopped' in the orchard before. I thought I'd never make it to the safety of my bedroom and for weeks I jumped whenever I saw a policeman. I would hide behind the garden wall so that he could not clamp the steel bracelets on my skinny wrists and carry me off. I gave up all thought of a life of crime.

When I was eight my sister Elise was born. I was disappointed that she was not eligible to join our gang, especially as she could not climb walls. We left her to her own devices and, as the months passed and her awareness grew, she became the willing, captive audience of our antics.

The time came eventually for me to move on to a well-regarded senior school and my burgeoning academic career sank without trace. I remember little of the school or of the teaching and only one incident remains vividly in my mind, causing me much embarrassment. It was the result of an art examination.

I was certainly not in the top two per cent of artists; nevertheless, I loved art lessons and my report cards said I was a 'trier'.

The Royal Academy of Art held optional examinations. I entered one and gained reasonable results. One morning after my bid for artistic stardom the art teacher sent for me. Her normally smiling face was serious as she handed me the results of my artistic endeavours on which was written, 'Is this intended as a joke?' Underneath this acid comment was a large 'F'. The subject matter was a bride and her two bridesmaids. The heavy paper was a dark colour which, to my mind, showed off to perfection the floating dress and veil of the bride as well as the dresses of her two minders. Before beginning I had agonised as to whether the picture would be more effective if the figures were shown front view or back view. Opting for the latter I set about my task and was very happy with the result. The bride was a blonde, the bridesmaids brunettes. 'Why did you do that?' I can clearly remember the teacher asking. Timidly I answered that I didn't think it mattered which way they faced. 'Not *that*,' she said. 'Why did you give the bride lime-green hair?' That was my first encounter with the drawback of being colour blind. The sad tale had a happy ending. The teacher re-submitted my picture with an explanation. After some weeks the slightly wilted bride (probably pregnant by then) and her attendants were returned to me, bearing a B plus.

At the ripe age of twelve years I was, like my mother, an avid reader, eagerly consuming every book I could lay hands on. School stories, the children's classics, adventures, the William books, nursing stories and, dare I say it, Enid Blyton, so frowned upon by school librarians, kept me enthralled. From the age of eight I had spent a lot of my spare time helping out in a private local library, contentedly licking an ice cream held in one hand and stamping the books with the other.

My parents were concerned about the sorry state of my education and suggested I might go to boarding school in England. My cousin was to attend the school as a day pupil and all my mother's family would be there to keep an eye on me. 'Would you like that?' they asked. Midnight feasts in the dormitory, great and dangerous adventures, tennis and lacrosse and, on top of all that, my first plane journey. Would I *like* it? I would *love* it.

The time dragged by. A large trunk with leather straps arrived, name tapes and uniforms were ordered. Again and again I admired the beautiful strings of the new tennis racket standing beside the equally pristine hockey stick and finally, just before I died of excitement, it was time to depart on the great adventure of my life.

At that time meat was still scarce in Britain, although it was quite plentiful in Ireland so, armed with a string bag packed with a huge piece of beef, several thick steaks and many other cuts of meat for my new-found relations, I was taken to the airport. My trunk, sports equipment and the string bag were loaded into the hold and I boarded the plane. My excitement masked my trepidation at leaving my family and I set off as proudly as many an explorer before me.

The journey went without incident for about fifteen minutes when the pilot announced that we would be returning to Dublin. 'Hooray', I thought, more flying.

An hour later the stewardess, who had finished her glamorous duty of serving tea and coffee, came and sat in the empty seat beside me. She told me all about her job which, I had already decided, was to be my future career. I asked the reason for the delay, and her answer brought the familiar flames to my cheeks. Two Alsatian dogs which were being transported in the hold had broken loose and were on the rampage ripping the luggage apart and generally creating havoc. We did not discuss the string bag stored in the hold alongside my school trunk!

My family had come to meet me and there was instant rapport between us. My grandmother, as colour blind as I am, was a great source of fun, and during my first term she took me out every Saturday for lunch and then to a film.

I was taken to meet the headmistress and, from that moment, began eighteen months of abject misery. The school had all the charm of a Dickensian workhouse. The headmistress was in her eighties, going on 300. I hated every minute of my time there and, most of all, I hated Sundays. Even on the hottest summer's day we marched along in a crocodile, clad in our grey hats, light coats and gloves, staring enviously at the happy, laughing children with their families. Back at school we had tea and then sat in a miserable, dark classroom sewing whilst a bored teacher read to us from the Bible.

Once my first term had ended I was no longer allowed my Saturday outings with my grandmother and had to make do with normal family visits. The one bright spot in the week was a visit to the cinema if, and only if, a 75 per cent mark was reached for the week's work. My marks shot up like a rocket. Not once did I miss the opportunity to escape into the magical world of film for three whole hours. Midnight feasts? Not a single one.

I was considerably younger than most of my class and had been allotted my own bedroom. No books in the dormitories or bedrooms was a strict rule, and it is thanks to a kindly matron that I did not run away when a severe cold kept me confined to bed for several days. She came into my sickroom to check on me and furtively produced a book from the depths of her crackling starched apron. It was *I Capture the Castle*, by Dodie Smith, my first adult novel. Having read it, I read it again. Twice daily during those few days of solitary confinement she slipped me books. She was more afraid than I was of being caught.

The Easter break was shorter than the usual holidays so my father arranged for me to join him in Manchester, where I met his side of the family for the first time. They were all warm and loving but I did my best to ruin his stay by pleading, every hour on the hour, to take me out of my awful educational prison. After a few days he realised that my homesickness was unbearable and, being a very soft-hearted man, he promised that if I completed the year, I could leave.

Would you believe it, when I returned home my family had moved! How many times have you heard that said jokingly? They did, however, give me the new address when they met me at the airport and took me to my new home. I vowed at that time that no child of mine would board at a school and my two never did.

The entrance examination for my new school presented no problem. Foolishly, I dropped Irish as a subject and this subsequently precluded me from passing my final examinations (Irish was a mandatory subject). Once again my work suffered as a result of my inattentiveness and I slid slowly down the academic ladder. My one claim to fame at that time was the 98 per cent I was awarded on the history paper in the 'mock' finals. Our history teacher knew how to make the subject come alive and she has left me with a life-long love of the subject.

At fifteen years of age I had completed my schooling. What next? My love of art was greater than my talent so it would have been a waste of time to go to art school. Instead, compromising, I applied to an academy of fashion. For years I had covered scraps of paper with sketches of outlandish and totally impractical fashions and felt that this might be my alternative to real art. One day, after I had sewn a piece of beige material with some green thread, I had to accept the fact that I was not going to become a great couturier and I left the colour sighted to their task. It is hard to think of a more ridiculous career for me to have chosen.

Next stop, secretarial college. This was a breeze; I enjoyed the funny squiggles of shorthand and the neatness of typing appealed to my eye. Bookkeeping was the third subject and something to be learnt even if not enjoyed.

Life was fun. The summer days always seemed to be warm and sunny as we waded through the usual teenage traumas. We supported one another through our devastatingly unhappy love affairs, the effects of which would last for at least two days. We laughed together at the ridiculous situations in which we found ourselves, one of which bears repeating.

A local swimming pool was our venue most days during these happy summer months. It was frequented by the young and the old (the young being fifteen or sixteen, the old, as much as twenty-two or twenty-three, really ancient). A friend and I were ambling home, I was (for a change) eating an ice cream, when we spotted a car approaching driven by a current heart-throb of mine. Beside him sat another Lothario of the moment, known to have caused a gleam in my friend's eye from time to time. How sophisticated can one be, wandering along covered in dripping mushy-vanilla? The only place to hide the childish cone was the book bag slung over my shoulder; I dropped it in. When we had practically walked under the car wheels to attract their attention the two Romeos offered us a lift. Once on board we recovered enough actually to speak to them but they were too busy eating ice creams to reply. Back home I opened my bag and found almost all the pages of all my books glued together. Whatever state must our stomach linings have been in? You may think that 'easy glue' is a recent invention – well, I have got news for you; it was invented years ago but they thought it was ice cream.

Towards the end of the summer I started work. That is to say, I worked for my father. With my up-to-date methods and new-found skills I set about reorganising his office. Within two days he handed me the car keys and told me to go swimming while he tried to find something, anything, in that modern, state-of-the-chaos office. Much as he loved me, I was driving him mad and, with no offence taken, I found another job – regrettably without swimming privileges.

Our local youth club was planning a visit to a summer school in England. My parents were taking my young sister on holiday and thought I would prefer the company of my own age group. Without any real enthusiasm, as none of my friends was going, I put my name on the youth-club list. I was not the only reluctant student at the school. David Schulman had been dragooned by his friends into attending the two weeks at Moreton Hall in Shropshire. It was at this school that I received my first bouquet of flowers. Romantic? Not really, it was from David and they were cauliflowers.

David lived in England. I returned to Ireland and during the next two years there was much to-ing and fro-ing. At the tender age of nineteen I walked up the aisle carrying, I am happy to say, a bouquet of real flowers. It is traditional for husband and wife to live together so I went back to England. Then, after a couple of years, we returned to settle in Ireland.

My parents retired and went to live abroad but, sadly, after only eighteen months of their happy retirement, my father passed away. My mother returned to live in Dublin and, I am glad to say, is still there.

The years rolled by; I was happy and busy at home with David and our two children. We learnt to play golf, played tennis and joined a squash club. We read and encouraged the children to do the same. Lynda was never without a book. Paul read in fits and starts, being more of an action-man. We did crosswords, puzzles and played games. I cooked and baked and became interested in the history of food.

We took the children to art galleries, museums, beauty spots, historical sites, zoos and the beaches. We had holidays at home and abroad. We felt they could not be too young to be exposed to the wonderful world of culture and art. We got our come-uppance the day we dragged them to the Guggenheim Gallery in New York. We wound our way down the spiralling walkway praising the varied and fascinating exhibits (but I must admit we could not explain all of them). At the end of our visit we asked our son Paul what he thought of it all. The angelic-faced four-year-old said it was a shame that they had messed up such a smashing skateboard slope with silly pictures. We placed culture on hold for him.

There were a lot of empty spaces on our book shelves left by books that failed to return home so I decided to stop being a lending library and started a book club. Twelve of us pooled money each month and one member in turn selected three books (always hardbacks). When everyone had read them they were returned to the original purchaser. The thirteen-year-old club is still in existence and in that time we have lost only one book.

A couple of even longer-standing clubs in our lives are the two poker 'schools' we joined. The men started theirs first and within weeks some wives, plus other volunteers, started their own game in opposition. We have been playing for over twenty years and to our shame, when the monetary system was decimalised, we did not follow suit and still play for pounds, shillings and pence (though at this stage more by tradition than conviction). One night the men's game ended rather later than usual. Counting the chips which they use in place of cash one of the players was three pounds twelve shillings and six pence down and, tired, wrote a cheque for the amount in old money. David, who is treasurer of the game, pocketed the cheque and the following day noticed the 'old-money' document. He presented it to the bank where it was honoured without question. The players never allowed him to forget his error, nor did they hear the comments of his fellow directors in the bank on which the cheque was drawn.

Both games are played for social reasons rather than for high stakes and the real winners over the years have been the various charities for whom the men collect a sum of money each week. Speaking for the ladies' game I can say we all look forward to it enormously. It is always fun and we have never had a contentious moment in all the time we have been together. We have quoted Shakespeare and cracked jokes – most of which were respectable. We have kept up with family news and, most surprisingly of all, we have never gossiped.

One night one of the ladies, utterly bored with her poor cards, proceeded to examine the workings of a miniature musical table. In the middle of a hand she placed the not-so-little box on the poker table in order to give it a more thorough inspection, all the time singing along with the tune. We could see neither the table nor the cards for some time as tears of laughter were streaming down our faces at the incongruity of it all. Sometimes, in the depths of winter, we have supplied cough drops for the ailing, in place of the usual sweets and chocolates. No player, however bad their coughs and sneezes, would dream of missing their night's entertainment. The only sad note has been the untimely loss of two of our players, both sorely missed. We discuss current affairs, television, recipes, politics, books, theatre and during these discussions play the odd hand or two of poker. The only time the conversation stops is when tea is served. Our distracted leader tries to keep us in order, vowing each week to leave us to our own devices, but we know that is only an empty threat. We have an official provider of paper tissues for the hilarious nights and another (the one who was so interested in the musical box) who supplies us with crystallised ginger which we eat gasping as we bluff our way to poverty. I also took up bridge and loved it; David already played.

Suddenly, out of the blue, the children were ready to fly the coop. I had lost my day job and Lynda insisted I should look for something positive to do. Paul agreed. David, always supportive, had no suggestions other than a possible adult education course. An arts course, maybe? I debated whether I should study again in order to obtain the necessary qualifications to apply for a university degree course. I put the decision on the long finger and simply got on with my life.

Some months later Harold Gale, British Mensa's executive director, called from Wolverhampton to speak to David. Mensa intended to start its own publishing company, he told me. I had spent ages searching without success for a puzzle book with work spaces and variety. I told Harold I thought there was a gap in the market for such a book. 'Compile one,' was his prompt reply. 'Submit it to the editor and if he does not consider it suitable he will tell you so.' I told him I would not know how to start. 'With a notebook and a pencil,' he replied, even more promptly this time. David came to take the call and I was left with food for thought.

Could I? Couldn't I? Should I? Shouldn't I? Lynda said, 'Try it.' Paul said, 'Go for it.' David said I had nothing to lose. I telephoned Robert Allen, editor at Mensa Publications, and he listened politely as I offered my expertise. I was very hurt that he would not agree to publish my book without seeing it first!

Settling down with books of facts, dictionaries, encyclopedias, three pencils (what extravagance), an art pad and a very large eraser, I set about compiling my first twenty puzzles. I drew them then rubbed them out, re-worded them then re-drew them. The paper became tissue thin so I did them again. At last they were ready. Would Robert accept them? I had a nerve-racking wait, then came the phone call – yes, he would.

The book was published and my greatest joy on seeing it was that I had managed to create something that was not simply to be eaten. Written into my contracts is the stipulation that the books must not be printed on rice paper.

A second and different one followed. This time I worked surrounded by builders' rubble and sand blasters, but it saved my sanity whilst our newly-built home was being replastered. I started a third book and my first sortie into fiction. This one was difficult because the story had to correspond with the puzzles; I was copying it by hand and errors were forcing me to scrap pages of writing in order to keep the drawings and story together.

A word processor? At one time I wouldn't have known where to begin, but, increasingly, 'I can't' was beginning to be replaced by 'I might' in my phrase-book. I succumbed. It was love at first byte. The day it arrived we had lunch at 4.30 p.m. David helped me rip the box open and set up my new miracle. I would become computer literate – or so I thought. We followed the manual carefully, set it all up and nothing happened. We tried again, still nothing. The disc was faulty and, feeling like disappointed children who had been given a toy without its battery, we switched off. 'At least when a pencil won't write you can sharpen it,' I grumbled.

Lynda, who by then was married and living in St Albans in England working in computers, phoned to see how things were going. It was a short call! We started again the following night, with a replacement disc and apologies from the suppliers, and were able to master the simplest of functions. Lynda phoned again. Would we like her to come over to help? We told her we would love her to come – regardless of her proposed help.

There is no truth in the rumour Lynda circulated concerning her arrival. We *did* allow her to take her coat off before leading her to the cream-coloured alien sitting on the table. She explained the various bewildering functions amid increasing hilarity and we ended up laughing hysterically as I botched things. Wiping my eyes I said, 'I bet you don't have that much fun with your clients.' Somewhat sardonically she informed me that as her firm charged £100 an hour for her time clients did not spend too much time laughing, and, in any case, by the time that they had to resort to paying that kind of money they were nearer to tears than laughter.

I could type and print out, spell-check, save information, but do precious little else. I might add that the word processor, in its wisdom, tried to rename several people when the text was run through the 'spell-check' option. Robert Allen became Robert Alien, Judy Hewitt (obviously a force to be reckoned with) became Judo Hewitt and the Executive Director of British Mensa must hang his head in shame – our old friend Harold Gale is known to my WP as 'Harlot'. I did not have time to sit down and go through the manual, so for three months every letter I wrote started with a black dot in the left-hand corner.

Wishing to spread my wings a little, I approached a publisher in Dublin and was delighted when they accepted and published a book of children's puzzles.

Then came the suggestion that I submit ideas for a light-hearted book about Mensa. I was quite unprepared for the reaction of the man I have idolised for thirty-six years.

'You are nuts, absolutely crazy,' he said, his elegant feet wobbling dangerously on their pedestal. Drawing myself to full height I kicked away the tottering column and shrivelled him with a glance and my erudite response – 'Why?' 'For heaven's sake, you don't know the first thing about the intricacies of the laws and by-laws, the constitution, the committee procedures, the testing methods worldwide – to name but three,' said the International Chairman. 'That', I answered, 'is a plus' (making a mental note to read the constitution). The look of a man who has just lost his wallet and his keys came over him; he accepted that his once greatest fan was going to write a book about Mensa and, with a hurried peck on my flaming cheek, he escaped to the sanity of his office.

In thirty-six years of marriage, with the exception of the eleven state-of-the-bean coffee makers I believed we could not live without, David had been supportive of anything I had ever wanted to do. His reaction made me nervous and, for a whole ten minutes, I was afraid he was right.

The invitation, request, suggestion – name it what you will – took me totally by surprise. The editor of Mensa Publications, a gentleman to his ink-stained fingertips, chose his words cleverly. 'You have a friendly approach to writing and people.' (no mention of literary genius), 'You have had the opportunity to see all sides of Mensa and you have not served on any committee, so your views are just those of a Mensa member.'

These gentlemanly observations, I assume, masked some omissions. Presumably, I would not cloud the issue with intellectualism, philosophy or any other 'osophies'. 'Let me have your ideas on how it might be written,' he said cautiously.

There were two avenues open to me: I could begin, 'It is propitious that one has been solicited to disseminate a narrative pertaining to this multifarious, Brobdingnagian, perspicacious, recondite aggregation in order to dissipate and juxtapose the opprobrious theory that Mensans are obdurate, hubristic illuminati', or I could simply state that I was going to try 'to prove that Mensans are normal people with one head, not necessarily of the egg-shaped variety'.

The first one I rejected as it would only have proved I owned a the-saurus. The second one was more my style. A couple of days later I received a copy of the editor's own book, *A Guide to the Art of Writing*, which soon convinced me that my decision had been correct.

For two days and nights, I click-clacked away on the keyboard (of the word processor, not the piano). Dinner was burnt one night and under-cooked the next. David eyed me – respectfully? Finally, with a flourish, I presented him with the first chapter and demanded that he read it. I watched his face. Thank goodness, his wallet and keys appeared to be intact.

My first job in writing this book was to find a suitable place for the avalanche of mail expected. I cleared two large shelves of the bookcase whilst wondering if I should warn our friendly postman of its impend-ing arrival. The *Mensa Magazine* had run a short article in its diary column inviting members to contribute their experiences or anecdotes, or both. I sat back and waited. Nothing happened. Suddenly, the avalanche began. Such excitement, one whole letter arrived, speedily fol-lowed, four days later, by another. Panic set in – what should I do? Was David right? Write to people, I reasoned – but would that do the trick?

I wrote letters to committee members, gifted children, Mensans I had met in Ireland, Britain and America, etc. and again I waited.

The American replies arrived almost by return of post; the information I sought was generously supplied together with offers of any further help if necessary. Three of the twenty-five gifted children I approached added their contributions and I received two anonymous letters. The first of these bore the address of the sender and contained a dreadful riddle which I shall repeat (why should I suffer alone?). Question: What do you call a group of Mensans travelling on the London Underground? Answer: A tube of smarties. And that was it.

Then realisation dawned: getting Mensans to write letters was like frying snowballs, so I took to the telephone. That opened up a whole new world. Everyone was happy to talk, give me anecdotes, share experiences and I scribbled away furiously as they recounted their tales. Wonderful – with one exception, I could not make head nor tale at times of my own notes. Sometimes, fascinated by the stories and their tellers, I listened and forgot to write. It did not take too long before I confessed to my illegible and disjointed notes and begged people to write to me. Some did, others just promised to. A further request, in the *International Journal*, and a larger article in the *Mensa Magazine* finally turned the famine into a feast; the responses poured in, begging to be read and placed on those now not-so-empty shelves.

Researching this book has been the most wonderful, frustrating, challenging and exhilarating experience. I have spent the best part of a year with Mensa and Mensans and feel I have not even begun to scratch the surface. I much regret having to leave out many of the letters, comments and communications I received, and only hope that I have managed to give a representative and not-too-serious picture of this wonderful society.

To the many, many unpraised and underpraised, hard workers of Mensa, I plead humility. To those who pick up their pens in order to correct factual errors, I plead senility. To those with even the slightest thought to litigation, I plead insanity. *Floreat Mensa.*